BLESS

THE.

MESSY

BLESS THE MESSY

LiFE LESSONS FROM A WORK iN PrOgreSS

JESS.BIRD

SIMON ELEMENT

NEW YORK   AMSTERDAM/ANTWERP   LONDON   TORONTO   SYDNEY   NEW DELHI

SIMON ELEMENT

An Imprint of Simon & Schuster, LLC
1230 Avenue of the Americas
New York, NY 10020

Copyright © 2025 by Jessica Antonow

First Simon Element hardcover edition June 2025

SIMON ELEMENT is a trademark of Simon &
Schuster, LLC

For information about special discounts
for bulk purchases, please contact Simon &
Schuster Special Sales at 1-866-506-1949 or
business@simonandschuster.com.

The Simon & Schuster Speakers Bureau can
bring authors to your live event. For more
information or to book an event, contact
the Simon & Schuster Speakers Bureau at
1-866-248-3049 or visit our website at
www.simonspeakers.com.

Manufactured in China

10 9 8 7 6 5 4 3 2 1

Library of Congress Cataloging-in-Publication
Data has been applied for.

ISBN 978-1-6680-2070-8

ISBN 978-1-6680-2071-5 (ebook)

FOR NAN.
EVERYTHING I AM IS BECAUSE
YOU HELD MY HAND THROUGH IT.
I OWE YOU EVERYTHING. I LOVE YOU.

FOR MILES & SAWYER.
YOU ARE MY LIGHT,
MY PURPOSE & MY JOY.
THANK YOU FOR YOUR
LIMITLESS LOVE.
♥

TABLE OF CONTENTS

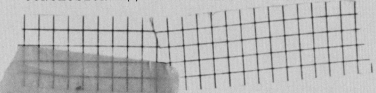

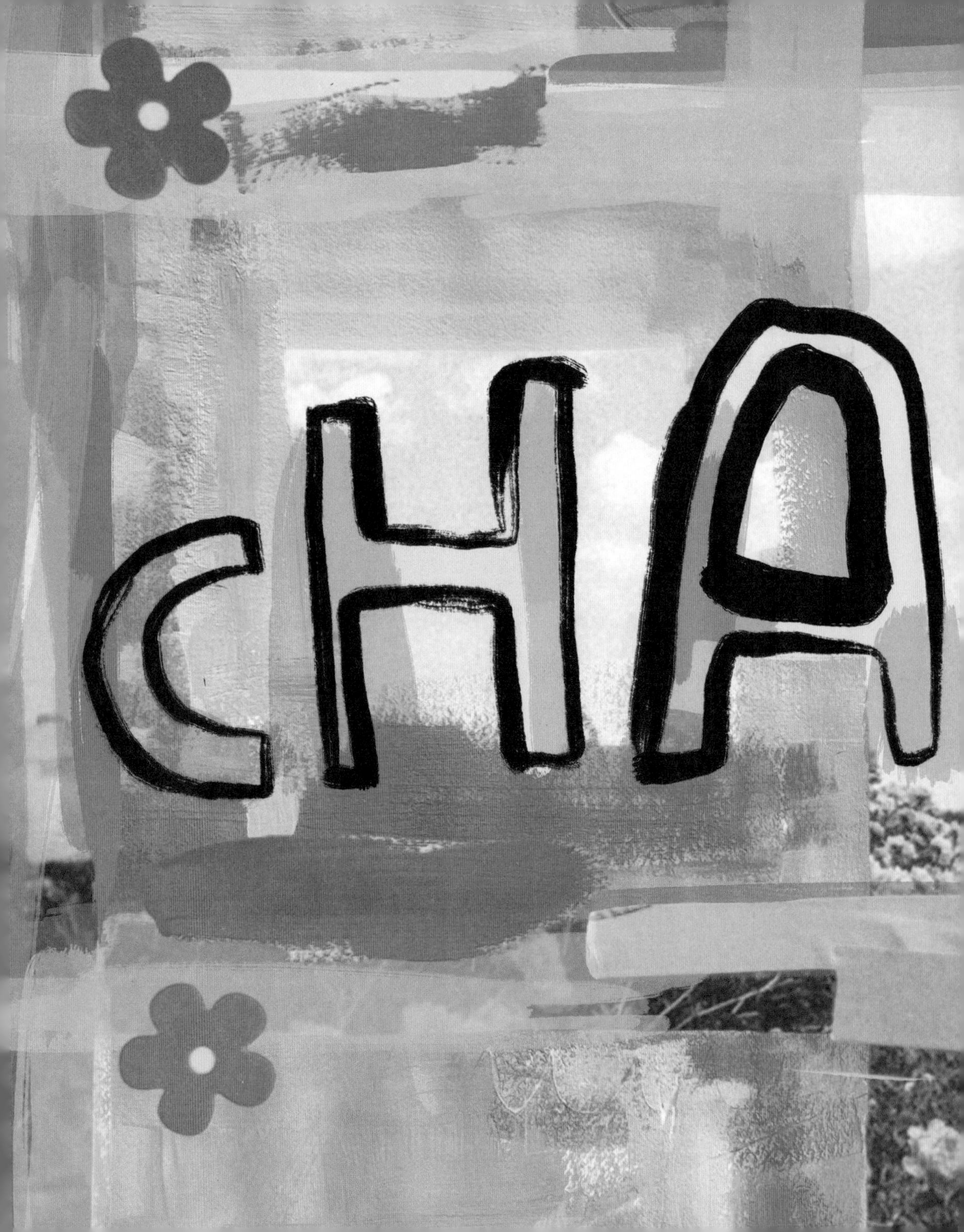
CHA

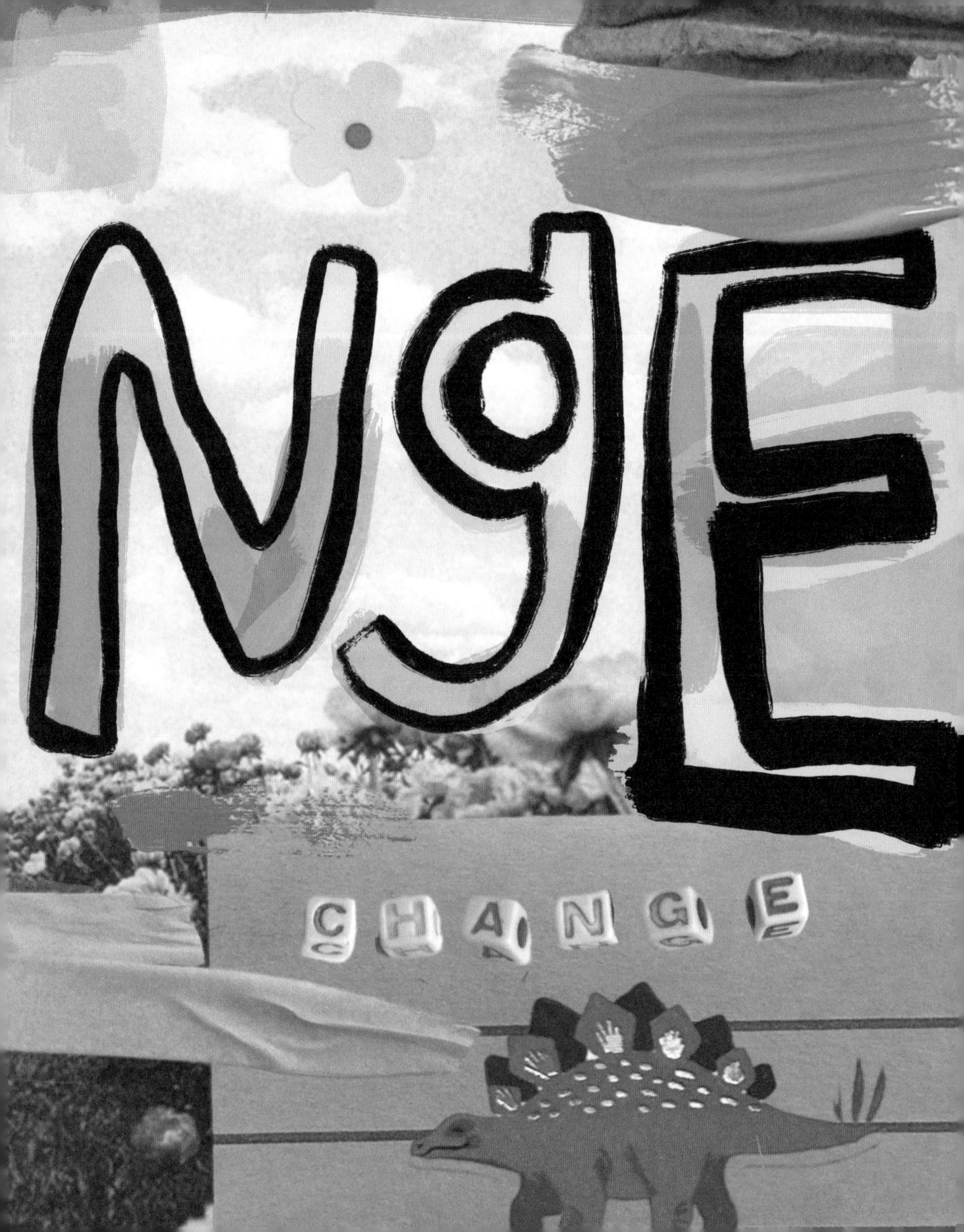
NgE
CHANGE

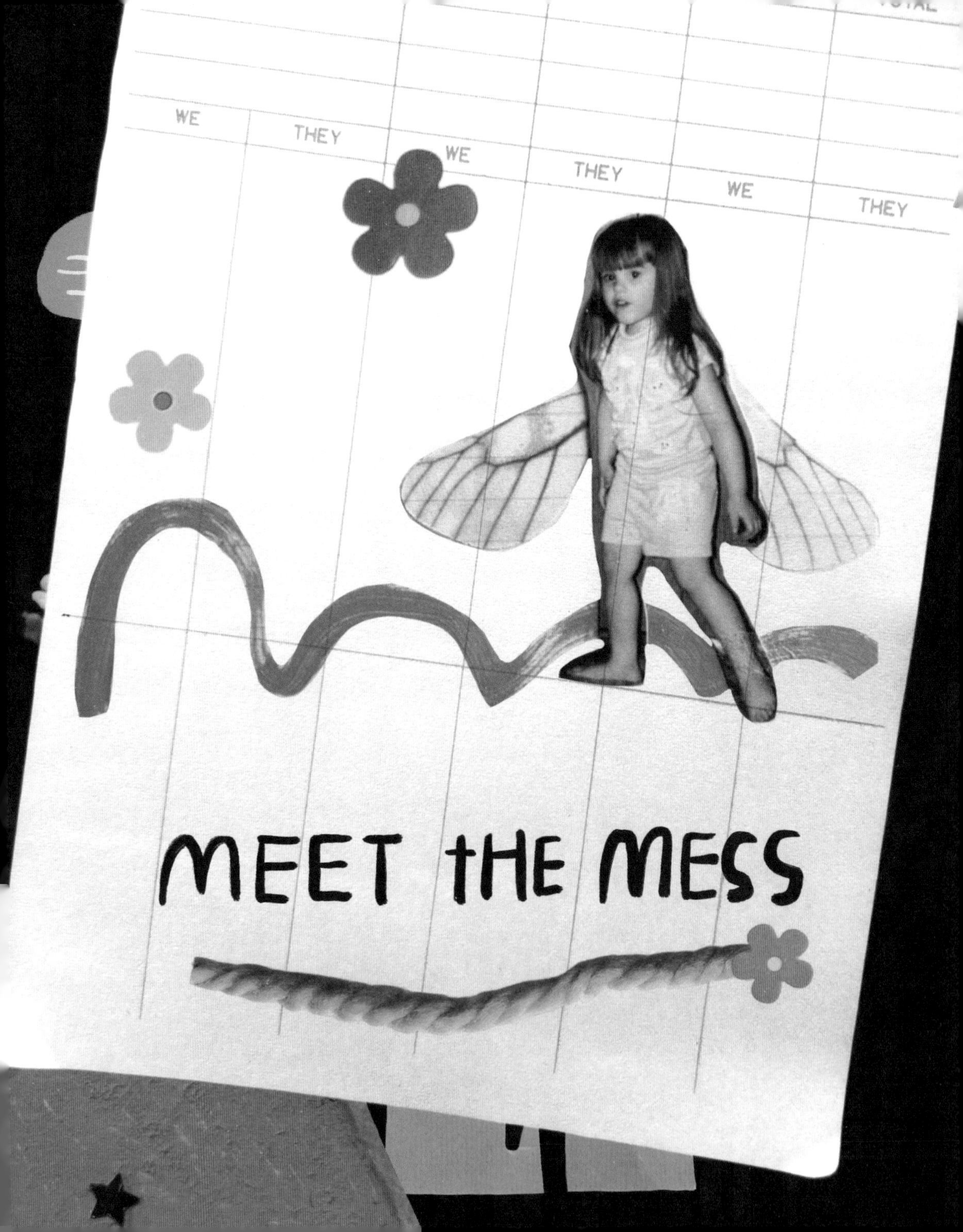
WE
THEY
WE
THEY
WE
THEY
MEET THE MESS

I am a mess. Understandably, this isn't normally something you would want to lead with or even self-proclaim, but we're going for transparency here, so I'll call it like it is. I wish I was just referring to *mess* in the emotional, metaphorical, chaotic life, sense, but I mean I am also an actual physical mess. There is almost always paint on my clothes or stuck in my hair. I have an array of coffee mugs and water glasses on my bedside table. When I open the hatch of my car, craft supplies will likely fall out. I am a mess. So it makes sense that my introduction to the world was rather chaotic. I don't even say that to be dramatic, just to be real. Some people can pinpoint a pivotal moment or event that made everything messy, but that's just what I was taught existence was.

I am the product of single mothers, low-income housing, and the free-lunch program. I am witness to drug abuse, domestic abuse, emotional abuse, sexual abuse. I am the child of adults who parentified me into a mother of both my siblings and them. I am the daughter of two men, one by blood and one by legality, who both decided I was too much for them. I moved from car to couch to apartment so many times growing up that I lost track and never felt a sense of safety in my

understanding of "home." I used food as a way to control and empty the pain from my being into the sink. I crash-landed in the world by way of a hurting girl who decided to keep her baby even though it wasn't in her plan (Mom, I know you did your best). I was championed and raised by Nan, my nana, who cut the cord of this stubborn Aries baby, and in so doing tethered us together for life.

My life has been a series of complex seasons of growing into myself. Some things have happened to me, and some things have been caused by my own affliction. And because I have become a superstar at masking everything going on beneath the surface, you will generally see me with a smile on my face even when it all feels yucky deep inside me.

My reality is that much of this book was written in the notes section of my phone. Wedged somewhere between a weekly grocery list and an endless reminder of to-dos for my kids are some of my deepest moments, thoughts, and feelings. And that's how I've always sort of existed—in the cracks of life. Fitting myself and my feelings into spaces that work for everyone else. Never wanting to disrupt the daily cycle but needing to shove the limitless loops of my mind somewhere. It's worked well enough over the years. It's not perfect but it's still good.

But maybe this book is where I finally take up space. Where my ideas and experiences pertaining to growth, healing, and becoming take center stage and are allowed to become as expansive and free as they wish to be. And that's the path that has led me here. One day I got on the silly social apps, and between the photos of my recent picturesque latte and another overly filtered selfie, I decided to be sincerely vulnerable about being deeply flawed and depressed. About not having it together. About really thinking about ending my life sometimes. About how I feel super alone. About being estranged from my parents. About going to therapy. About being gay but married to a man. That's what brought me to this book, and to you.

Listen, I tell everyone I am an expert in nothing but my own experience. I am not a therapist or a doctor or even someone with a college degree (which is a huge insecurity of mine that we can chat about later). I'm just a person who has been through a bunch of shit and wants other people to maybe go through less shit

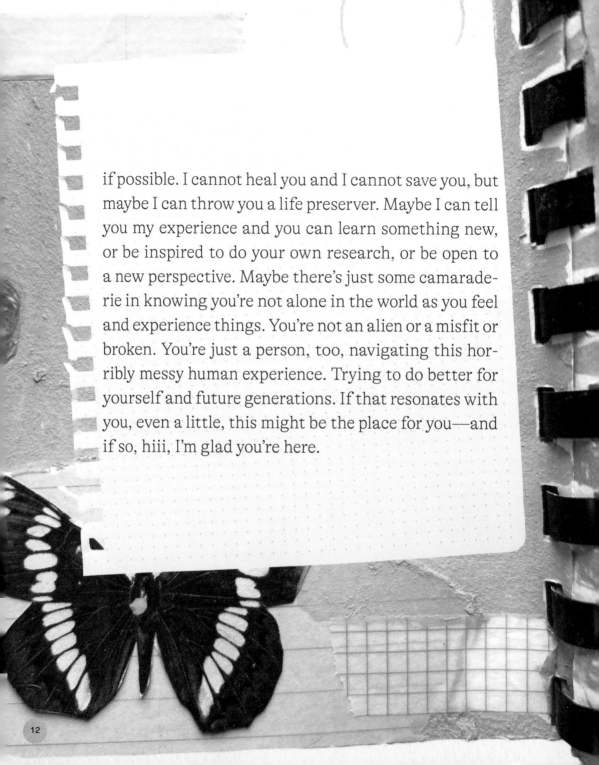

if possible. I cannot heal you and I cannot save you, but maybe I can throw you a life preserver. Maybe I can tell you my experience and you can learn something new, or be inspired to do your own research, or be open to a new perspective. Maybe there's just some camaraderie in knowing you're not alone in the world as you feel and experience things. You're not an alien or a misfit or broken. You're just a person, too, navigating this horribly messy human experience. Trying to do better for yourself and future generations. If that resonates with you, even a little, this might be the place for you—and if so, hiii, I'm glad you're here.

it's okay to start over & live a life you're proud of.

remember,

WE ALL BLOOM in OUr OWN timE.

trust tHE PROCEss.

LAtE BLOOMEr

I'm gonna level with you: I am a chronically late person. Be it the time blindness from my ADHD, my inability to ever like the way my clothes feel, or the paralyzing social anxiety that makes me not want to leave the house, I am absolutely the friend who tells you I'm "on the way" when I'm soaking wet in my bedroom post-shower trying to pick the right music vibe to get ready to. But even with my incurable lateness, I can surely promise you that the one thing I did not ever expect to be late for was living my own life. But there I was at twenty-nine years old, sitting across from my brand-new thera-pist with my legs pulled up on her small blue couch that I wished could engulf me whole, weighing the mass of total honesty against the consequences of reality.

I wasn't new to therapy. I had been in and out of these offices since I was in the fourth grade, but, like many other things, I learned to acclimate to the envi-ronment. Being "good" at therapy became a résumé addition for me. Saying just enough to be vulnerable, to make enough progress, and, most important, to get my ego a gold star for healing and overcoming so much. Being resilient became a merit badge I proudly wore.

I saw it as an accolade of goodness, of strength, to be this kid who had been through some shit and was somehow still a worthwhile person.

But I knew that day if I wanted a real shot at not being depressed forever, lying on floors staring at the ceiling with Bright Eyes songs reverberating off the walls, I was going to have to give up my armor of resilience and the parts of me that would rather get a pat on the head than deal with the stuff that kept me up at night with ideations playing in my mind.

I stared at the plants lining the windowsill for a long while, then took a deep breath and spoke shakily. "I have a nearly perfect life. I'm married to a good man. I have two magical tiny humans. I have loads of friends. I'm *mostly* happy. But I still think about killing myself almost every day. . . . I'm pretty sure it's because I'm gay." I remember how calm my therapist was; there was no indication on her face or in her body language that she didn't believe me. I've spent the majority of my life feeling like I was crazy. Most of the people around me even unintentionally confirmed this by assuring me that I

couldn't trust myself or my emotions. But my therapist sat there with a warmness I remember believing. She had a pink streak under her ear in her short wavy hair, she wore sweaters that told you she was well traveled, and she had wrinkles by her eyes that assured you she had lived life well. From the moment the words fell out of my mouth, a shift began within me. I thought this self-revelation was enough to keep me grounded and to continue living life on its regularly scheduled program. All I needed was to be honest with myself, right? I truly believed it was a secret I could keep—that knowing my truth would ease the discontentment in my body and mind and I could just die being the person everyone already loved, the person they knew and trusted. To my people-pleasing soul, the idea of willingly blurting out something that would likely not be celebrated and would shift my entire ecosystem just seemed absurd.

Why would I willingly go through pain? Why also would I willingly put people I loved through pain? That seemed ridiculous and uncomfortable, and instead I could just sit on my couch after my babies went to sleep, draw in my sketchbook, and watch *Gilmore Girls* for the nine-hundredth time through. That seemed like an entirely more logical and unadventurous option for me. Plus, how hard could holding a secret about your entire identity be? That would absolutely not backfire or internally crush me. I'd probably be fine!

But, no, dear friends, I would not be fine. Actually, I would be worse, and I would do things I still regret to people I deeply cared for. I'm still working through a good amount of sadness and shame about those decisions, and I wish I could have avoided some of those painful consequences.

Living seemed like a blur of dismantling the life I had built while stepping forward to build a new one. And it hurt; it really fucking hurt. It was a Venn diagram of internal euphoria and complete external hell. It was excruciating.

Coming out was the first time I ever chose myself.

It's unbelievable to me that it took thirty years to quiet all the voices, and the expectations, and the people-pleasing, and the need to be loved by every single person and just maybe love my damn self.

It felt simultaneously terrifying and liberating.

Now all I had to do was figure out how to tell everyone else.

I know many people were probably shocked when I came out because (1) they told me so to my face, (2) they said they were perplexed that I had "never hit on them," which honestly made me laugh, and (3) I had never given any outward indication that I might be gay. By that I knew they meant that I had always had a boyfriend—like, serial-relationship-haver boyfriends. Like very skinny long-haired boys who played guitar–type boyfriends. But I also had severe daddy issues and thought that the only way to have worth was for a man to choose you. So, I let myself get chosen and discarded and chosen again, feeling more and more with each disposal that the recurring problem was me. I lost my virginity when I was fifteen to a boy who was eighteen. My mother let him sleep over in my room, even though I really wish she would have established some rules and bound-aries. I didn't feel safe, but I felt chosen, and at that time I thought those feelings were the same thing. So I became good at being physical because it seemed like being physical got you more attention, which made you feel more chosen. I didn't enjoy this part, but I deeply valued the commitment and the holding and the idea that maybe a man could stay and love me. So who really cared if I had to do those sexual things I sort of hated? They were just stepping stones to the part I desperately needed: to be wanted. To be worth showing up for. To be loved.

In my late teens I found a loophole to the whole sex situation by way of Christian boys. Christian boys were a nice respite because they were saving themselves for marriage, so the sex part was (to my relief) off the table. We could cuddle and kiss, and maybe if I was lucky I could even dry hump my way to an orgasm. And that was all perfectly lovely for me. I got my commitment and my love and didn't even have to take my clothes off.

But dating Christian boys introduced me to an entirely new culture: organized religion. I can remember sitting on the floor of a friend's bedroom in a house on a wealthy suburban cul-de-sac the first time a boy I liked invited me to church. It was proposed as another way we could see each other that week and hang with some friends.

I had never had anything to do on Sundays anyway, so the idea of seeing him felt great. Sure, church . . . how bad could that be? I had sat through my fair share of

Italian American Catholic masses by that point, so I felt I could handle the whole church thing. You go, sing some old songs to organ music, sit-stand-kneel-sit, and then go out to lunch after. I figured I could sit through his church service to get to the lunch part easy-peasy. But I don't think I could ever have been ready for what awaited me in the awkwardly shaped brick building that looked like a child's careless Lego construction. It was as if I'd been transported to another dimension where love was (seemingly) given freely. Where you were told you were intentionally perfectly created. Where it was believed that we were all family. *Family? Love? Not being a mistake?* This was everything I'd been wishing for my entire life. I followed the white rabbit down the hole hard. I once told my therapist that I truly feel that ten years in the grasp of organized religion taught me to hate myself more than my toxic upbringing, because I never thought I was a bad person growing up. I thought bad things happened around me, I thought maybe I wasn't dealt great cards, but never until I drank the Kool-Aid of religion did I think I was inherently broken and bad and unworthy.

UNRAVELED

Let's be honest—y'all are nosy. I mean, I think we all are, at least a little, right? We want to know the story. The tea. The 411 (for those of us who are over thirty-five). So I can't be surprised that people are often interested in knowing how the hell a closeted queer was able to make it into a marriage with a man and stay married for so long.

Welp, it's honestly not as crazy as you think. Take a childhood full of trauma, a crippling need to live up to societal expectations, a heap of internalized homophobia, and a spread of late-teen religious trauma. It's a fairly simple recipe.

But I have to add in the fact that I genuinely liked the person I was married to. Of all the straight white men in the world, he was a really good one, and, honestly, for years he was my best friend. And that made the pieces that didn't fit less noticeable.

It's like your favorite sweater with the hole in the armpit. It's still wearable. It feels right, it's comfortable,

I HOLD SPACE FOR ALL THE VERSIONS OF MYSELF & KNOW EACH OF THEM DID THE BEST THEY COULD WITH WHAT THEY HAD AT THE TIME.

things can be different and still be okay.

it's cozy. You know the hole is there, but most of the time no one else can see it.

But over time the hole gets bigger. You may even start to notice other things beginning to fray. Snags. Loose threads. A few lost buttons.

Then, suddenly, one day you pull it out and know it's not even wearable anymore.

That's what happened to my marriage.

It was my comfort item. I could ignore the holes because it still fit well enough. But as we grew up and grew into ourselves, the gaps got bigger and it began to unravel. And our marriage just wasn't wearable anymore.

NOTES ON LETTING GO & Living AuTHENTicALLy

The more we let go of our need to be liked, the more we step into the opportunity of being loved as a more authentic and sincere person. Needing to control what others think about you only limits your ability to show up as yourself. Most of my life I teetered between being loudly myself and working hard to blend in and be accepted. The need to be well-liked often kept my inner weirdo at bay. I vividly remember how excited I was when I found this bright yellow trench jacket at a GAP outlet while shopping with my nana. It was long, lightweight, and had a blue-and-green polka-dot lining. Somehow it was on sale for $15.99. I persuaded Nan that I needed it, and she gave in. I wore it to school as a statement piece over my denim jeans, tight white tee, and hoop earrings. Wearing something outré wasn't new to me: I loved to play with fashion, dye my hair, and upcycle my clothes. But on this day a guy in my

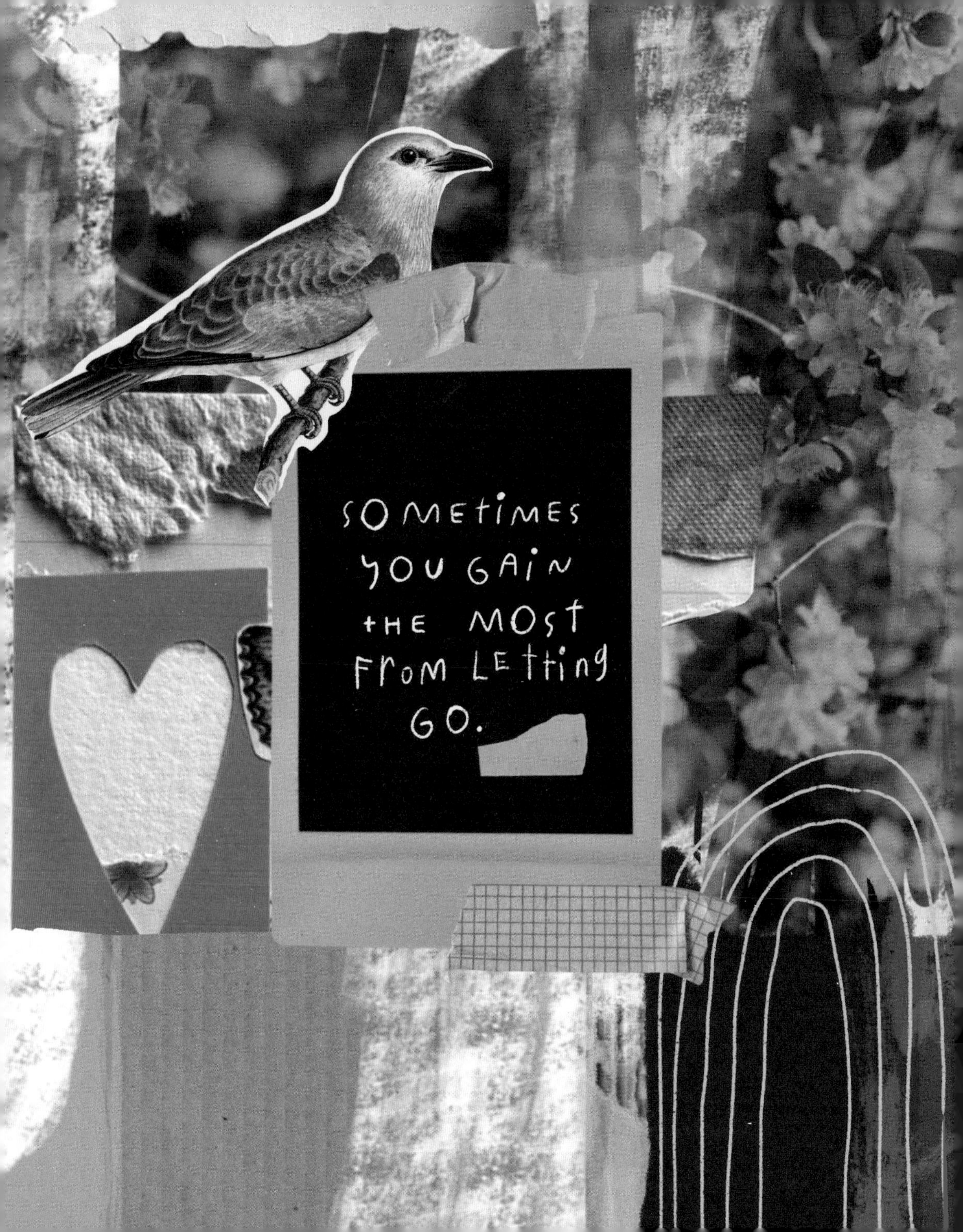
SOMETIMES
YOU GAIN
THE MOST
FROM LETTING
GO.

REMINDER:

LiVING AUTHENTICALLY
WiLL ALWAYS COST YOU
PEOPLE WHO ARE STiLL
HiDING FROM
THEMSELVES.

tenth-grade history class said, "Jess, why do you do that? You look good, and then you put something weird like this over it and ruin it. You would be so hot if you were just normal."

I think I've been chasing some idea of normal my entire life. Trying to figure out how to be *me* and how to be liked, because having both seemed nearly impossible. I'm learning to live my life vibrantly, without regard for the way others decide to view me. I will not and cannot live my life for them; I have to live it for me. Let your inner weirdo free. Be unapologetic in your authenticity. Grow, GROW! Even if it's not in a way those around you expected or hoped.

PLOT twist

This book started out as something completely different. The themes and experiences might be similar, but overall, the book you're reading is a different book than the one I set out to write. I started writing thinking it would be only a few months until I was turning this in, but instead I was crying on a Zoom call with my agent and editor after a recent suicide attempt, changing dates and timelines to make more sense with my changing life. And that's how fast it can happen, how fast your story can change. What was once meant to be the entirety of this book is now just an excerpt. What once were things I thought I knew now seem much more complex as my understanding of myself has evolved. There are also hard lessons I've learned twice or thrice over at this point, and they hurt just as badly as the first time I learned them. Clarity comes with all these things, and the only thing I'm extremely clear on is that change is constant. Knowing and accepting that will give you peace.

SOME PAINFUL THINGS CLEAR YOUR PATH.

tiny rituALs
fOR stARtiNG AGAiN

MAKE yOUr BED

OPEN tHE WiNDOWS

BUy A FRESH JOURNAL
(& PENS!)

tAKE A WArm sHOWER

DUALiTY

Making sense of feelings can be a lot.

Our feelings are often confusing. What can catch us even more off guard is when there are multiple feelings fighting for our attention. How can we feel two feelings that strike us as, notably, conflicting feelings at the exact same time? It can make us feel crazy, but that, my friend, is duality. The act of existing in two spaces at one time. It doesn't make one feeling more or less true. It just means they both are present in a certain experience. Remember, you're a complicated, intricate baddie who contains multitudes. It's a good thing. Don't ever be ashamed of your ability to feel many things. It's a gift.

you are
allowed
to
evolve

(AND it CAN BE DIFFERENT
THAN OTHERS EXPECT)

EVOLViNG CAN LOOK LiKE:

- CHANGING YOUR MiND
- CHANGING YOUR CAREER
- CHANGING YOUR BOUNDARIES
- CHANGING YOUR POINT OF VIEW
- CHANGING YOUR HAIRSTYLE
- CHANGING YOUR DREAMS

EVERYONE'S growth LOOKs DiFFErENt

Society has set us up to constantly compare ourselves to one another, to always look next to us instead of looking inward. Scrolling through screens, seeing everything from extravagant vacations we wish we were on to relationships we wish we had to products we are influenced to desire. Capitalism breeds a constant cycle of wanting what another has by reminding us of our lack, then selling us things we believe might be able to hide the holes in our soul.

Inner growth and healing work are not quantifiable, photographable moments you can post in a reel of shared images in hopes of validation (which, I promise you, is fleeting). Sometimes they are immense, beautiful moments that everyone can see, cheer for, and revel in, times we feel in full bloom and want others to see what we've accomplished and who we've become. But

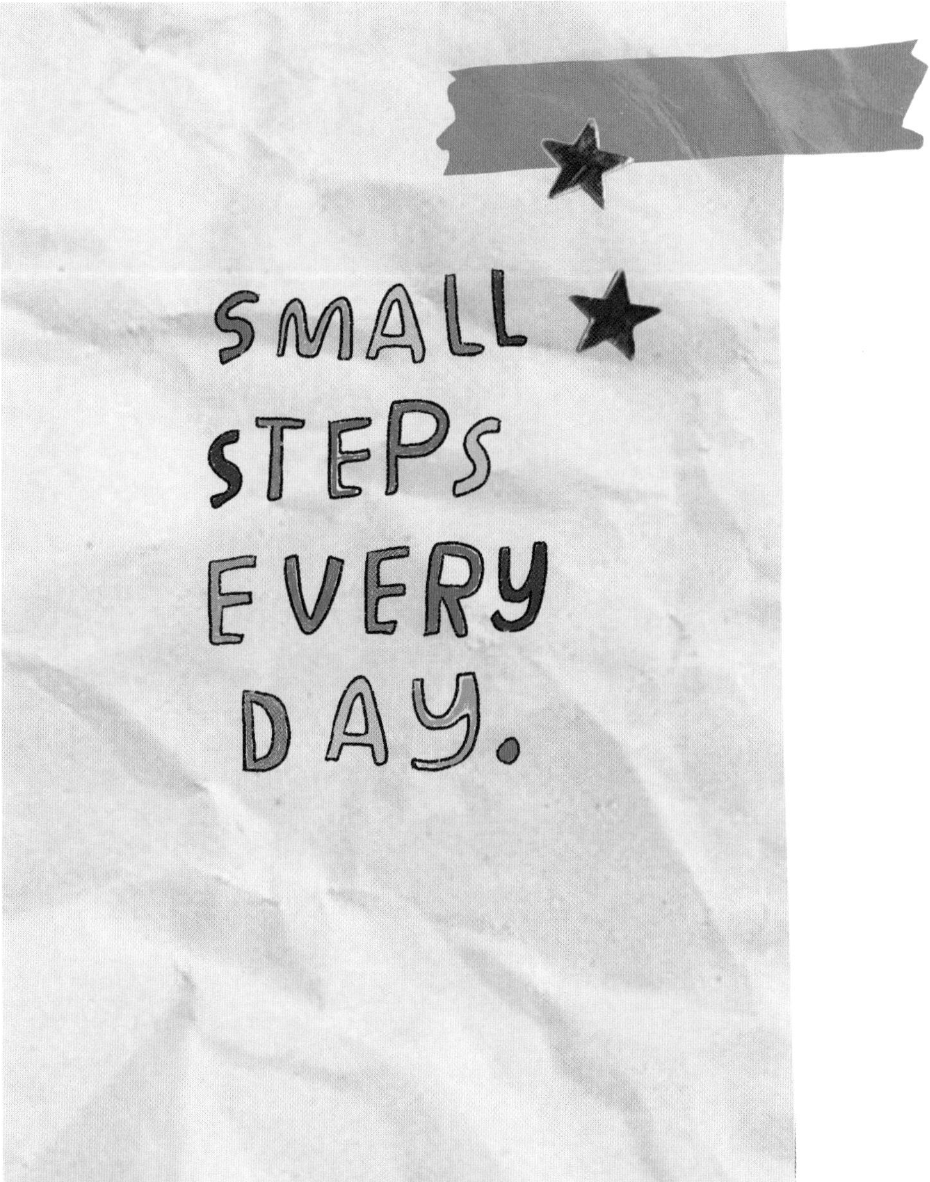
SMALL
STEPS
EVERY
DAY.

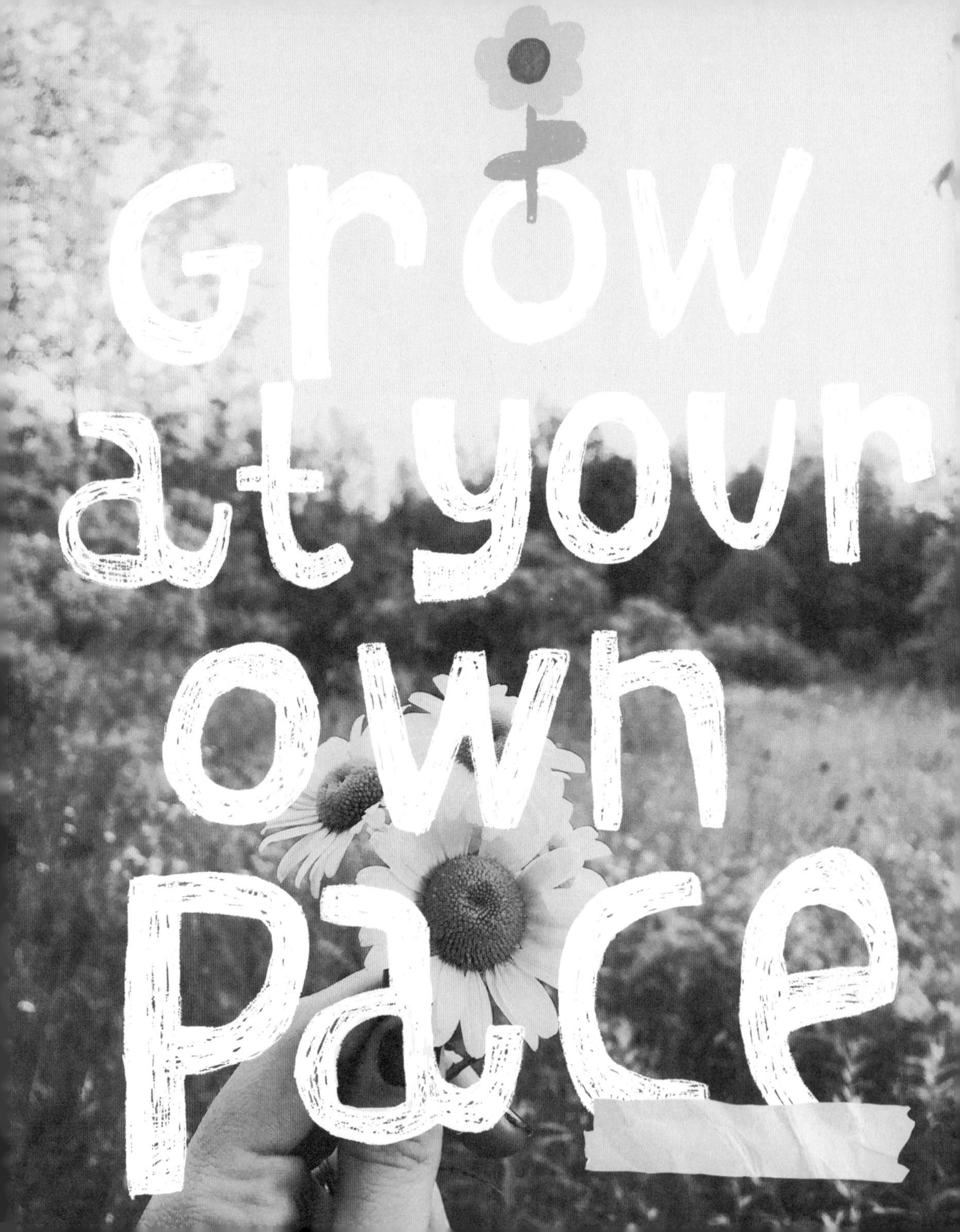
Grow
at your
own
pace

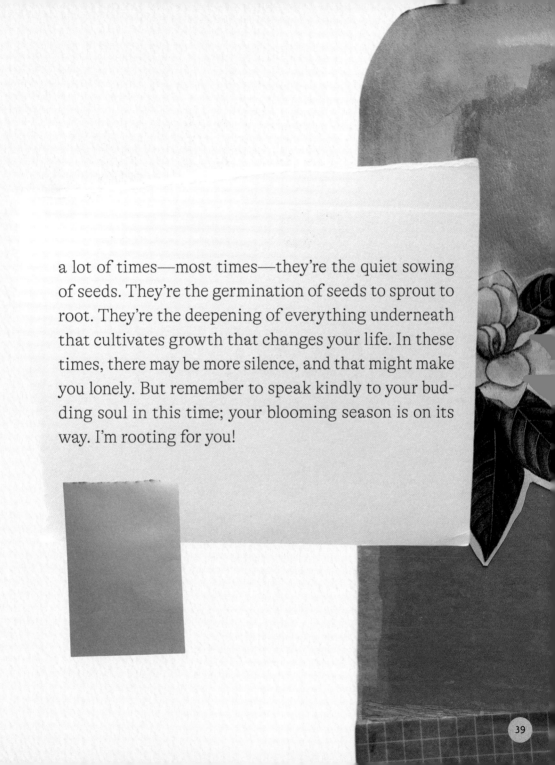

a lot of times—most times—they're the quiet sowing of seeds. They're the germination of seeds to sprout to root. They're the deepening of everything underneath that cultivates growth that changes your life. In these times, there may be more silence, and that might make you lonely. But remember to speak kindly to your budding soul in this time; your blooming season is on its way. I'm rooting for you!

FEEL it to HEAL it.

It might seem self-explanatory and elementary to be encouraged to feel your feelings, but you would be shocked by how often we think we're feeling our pain but are actually just observing it. We may acknowledge it, but then we numb ourselves as a way to self-protect. That only keeps the pain locked inside, causing it to build. Feeling is understanding. Feeling is the only way we can release the discomfort and begin to heal. Feelings, however painful, are not forever. They are visitors. Allow them in, affirm them, and then let them go on their way. Try to listen for the reason for the feelings' visit—what are they trying to tell you? Teach you? Protect you from?

FEELINGS ARE JUST VISITORS

greet them with gentleness & then let them go.

JOurnALiN9 101

Journaling has been part of my life since I got a rain-bow kitten Lisa Frank diary for my seventh birthday. Writing my feelings down was always a way I could communicate and make sense of things in my world. I never thought it would be a lifelong practice. It wasn't always safe to say the things I wanted to or needed to in my environments growing up, so I wrote them in my journal instead. My journaling has evolved with me over the years, and I still find it a gift to have a chroni-cle of my personal experiences, growth, and becoming. If you've ever considered journaling or thought about picking it back up, here is your push.

There is no right or wrong way to practice this pro-cess. It might feel awkward as you begin to share your-self in this way. Maybe you'll write every day. Maybe it will be on an as-needed basis. Try not to put unneces-sary pressure on the process. Journaling is meant to be a helpful tool, not another reason for you to feel crappy about yourself. Make it art, make it ritual—just make it yours.

BENEFITS of JOURNALING

★ CLEARS & CALMS your MIND

★ CREATES SELF-AWARENESS

★ IMPROVES MEMORY

★ HELPS TO SET GOALS & track progress

★ HELPS REMIND YOU HOW FAR YOU'VE COME

★ BOOSTS MOOD & SENSE OF WELL-BEING

IT MIGHT FEEL LIKE YOU'RE giving UP BUT MAYBE YOU JUST KNOW WHEN IT'S TIME TO MOVE ON.

SOME
LOSSES
YOU
WILL
FEEL
MANY
TIMES.

it's OKAY if you STILL FEEL AN ACHE or sadness WHEN yOu cHOOSE WHAt's BEST FOR YOU.

LANCE-LEAVED COREOPSIS

BEING IN "THE FEELS"

Just a reminder that it's okay to feel sad after making the right decision for you. Choosing what's best for you doesn't necessarily mean there won't be pain and sadness tied to it. Sometimes the things we choose to protect ourselves, heal ourselves, and free ourselves still need a hefty mourning process. It might be grieving the loss of a relationship, the loss of an idea, the loss of a trajectory to somewhere you assumed you were headed. Remember that feelings are not meant to be fixed; they're meant to be felt. Feeling that pain doesn't mean the decision wasn't the right one; it just means you're human.

Learn to love yourself through the losses. Your progress doesn't always and will not always be validated or understood by others. You must be able to validate yourself. You must be able to stand behind your decisions, because they are yours. Be your own cheerleader, your own hype person, your own fan.

cut it BACK

Plants have always inspired me; they are my teachers. I bought my first plant on a whim eight years ago for $11.99 and have never looked back. As I listen to and care for my plants, I learn so much about my own healing. Did you know that when you cut away part of a plant, it shifts the resources to healthier, thriving parts of the plant? And I'm not just talking about cutting off the dead and decaying parts; I'm talking about a full pruning of leaves that may otherwise look healthy but you know are not growing at the rate they should. They're taking away from the overall growth; they're slowing the plant down; they're keeping it from really flourishing. I see that there are things that need to be cut away as I continue to evolve and expand in my own becoming. Habits, relationships, self-views, mindsets, emotions, and anything else that is keeping you from propelling yourself forward. It's hard to see sometimes: Some leaves look healthy, so why remove them? Because you were not made to be everything to everyone. It's okay to save your energy for the spaces of your life that deserve it.

i HOPE YOU FiND PEACE WiTHiN YOURSELF.
TITLE
NAME
DATE RETURNED

tiny rituALs

fOR outGROwiNG FRiENDshiPs

mOurn As NEEDED
(it's oKAy to miss tHEM)

rEPAiNt A SPACE iN your HOUSE

rEPOt yOur PLANts to giVE tHEM MOre rOOm to grOw

PAUSE

Make sure you take moments to stop, look around, and breathe in where you are right now. Sure, that sounds like a line from a greeting card—I hear you—but I mean it. Sometimes we get so caught up in our healing that we don't take stock of how far in the rebuilding process we have truly come. Remember when you didn't know how to say no without overexplaining yourself, and now your boundaries are stable as hell? Remember when that trigger would ruin your whole day, and now it's just a passing thought? Remember when you didn't know your own voice, and now your presence and inner peace allow you to actively take up space? Yeah. Those are, like, *huge* things. Don't get so caught up in getting there that you forget that the process is where you will see yourself really start to transform. Find pockets of delight throughout the in-between— maybe even enjoy it!

HONOr tHE SPACE

4

BEtWEEN WHERE
YOU ArE

AND WHERE YOU
WILL BE.

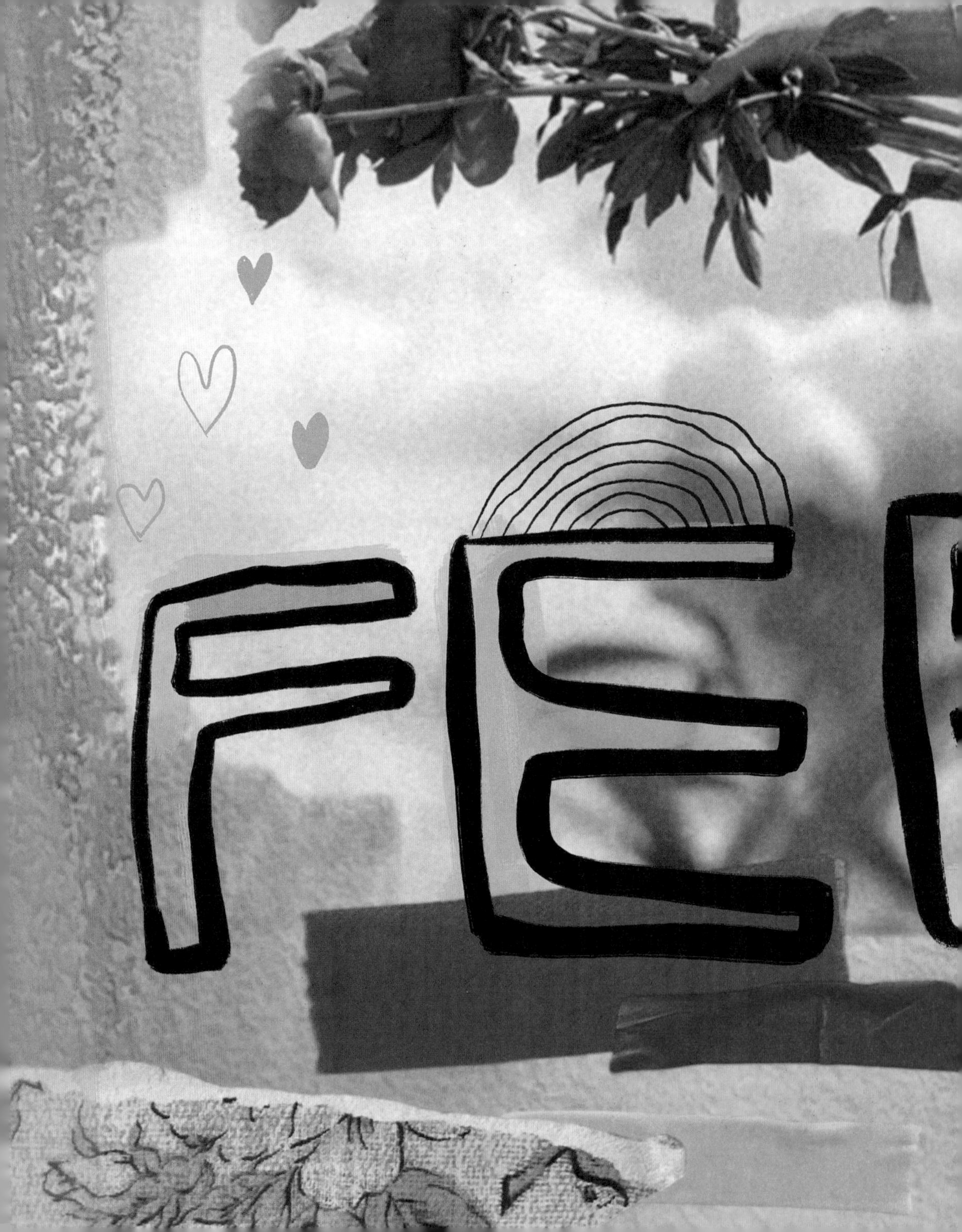
FE

BOARDI

006 2224
HCIG
FLYR

DEPA

DLXXXXX1650

VKX26NBL
FLIGHT   DATE   CLASS   ORIGIN

DL2   09APR   E   LONDON-HEATHROW10
OPERATED BY   BASIC   DESTINATION   BRD
DELTA AIR LINES INC   NY -KENNEDY   9

start
SOME-
WHERE

ErAs

It's funny: when a new era of your life starts, it doesn't always feel monumental. Yes, some cycles are sharp turns and deep dives and total makeovers, but some may just be a quiet untangling of the knotted chain that was who you were. One day you might be standing in your kitchen, making your morning coffee, looking out the window, and you might feel it: the shift. The realization of how far you've come from where you were, and maybe (for once) the feeling of excitement for the things you may still have to discover. Seasons are passing, but eras are distinct moments in time. They represent you—old you, new you, the you that is still in process. Eras are odes to us. They are the landmarks we can recount when we talk about our story and connect to others. Don't rush your eras. Some might seem silly, like "the era of the blond streak," and some will change you forever, like "the era of finding my voice."

DECIDING to LIVE
is ONE oF THE
BrAVEST
THings you
cAN DO.

SOME-
TIMES
UNKNOWNS ARE
INVITATIONS
to SELF-
TRUST.

BEING ABLE to sit in YOUR FEELINGS is ESSENTIAL to a CALM NERVOUS SYSTEM.

leaf hopper

cicada

SELF-LOVE sHit

So you made the conscious decision your life needs to change, but you might not know where start. You look around and start to see things for what they are and what they were and must choose a way forward. As RuPaul says, "If you can't love yourself, how in the hell you gonna love somebody else?" And while self-love might not come easy to us, it's a good place to start. Self-love made its way into the circle of overused buzz-words to sell you a bunch of garbage you probably don't need to achieve it. But self-love is also a crucial part of becoming your most authentic self. Maybe it's not as easy as it's assumed or fed to us by the media to be, because if you were never shown love, how do you know what love looks like? Many of the ways we love are just a reflection of how we were loved. So, like all good things that are worth figuring out, self-love takes practice.

To me, self-love *is* a practice, a habit, a thing that requires consistent commitment. I was possibly self-love's biggest advocate—although I wasn't actually an active participant myself. And while I haven't gone pro

DON'T SABOTAGE YOUR CURRENT PEACE BECAUSE you're more comfortable iN CHAOS.

or anything, I can at least (after multiple years of therapy) say I deserve love and, even more, that I might even know I love myself. Much of this comes with learning to sit with ourselves long enough to find out what might have stopped us from accepting love or the idea that we are lovable.

I KiNDA HATE THE WOrD FOreVEr

"Till death do us part" is maybe romantic on some level, but for someone who really values their autonomy and hates committing to plans even for later the same day, it can feel . . . stressful. The first time I got married, I said the "forever" things and I really freaking meant them. In my mind, getting divorced equaled failure, and I was not a quitter. But that extreme level of tethering yourself to someone also doesn't leave a lot of room to grow and evolve as a human (especially when you're getting married at twenty-four like I was). I know the hope is that you both will change in perfect harmony so there will be no need to separate—meaning you have to do it at a pace that works for you *and* keeps your partner in sync. But what if you don't? Do you stay unfulfilled or become a failure? Are those the options? I think forever is a very long time. I think the world shifts and moves, and although we're all desperate for something concrete and stable, the truth is we must be open to the fact that we really cannot control what "forever" will look like. Since my main goal in marriage was to not get divorced, I dug my heels so far into the ground that I distracted and disassociated myself into an extremely scary place—because I wanted to do what was "right."

I'm learning that what's "right" in societal standards is not always right for me. Because I'm going to tell you a controversial idea about my marriage to my kids' dad: I do not think it failed, not even one little bit. I've come to understand that not only are there stories of our lives but there are also volumes. The book that contained my first marriage is over, but a new volume has begun. The story is not over. Life is an entire series of different books and evolutions of ourselves. And this doesn't mean the story is devoid of sadness. It just means it goes on, and yours can, too. You can finish one book and still have limitless potential to write another. A fresh start is scary—I get it; I can barely commit to starting a new sketchbook. But something happens when you give in to a new beginning: you realize that even if you fill these pages with nonsense and scribbles, there can be another book after that, and another after that. Nothing is ever wasted; it is simply being formed. Never stop writing your story. You deserve all the space and all the pages.

DON'T STAY IN YOUR COMFORT ZONE.

it will HOLD YOU BACK FROM WHO YOU ARE MEANT TO BE.

it's OKAY
to FEEL
tHINGS
DEEPLY.

Feeling tHings DEEPLy

I was mocked as a kid for feeling deeply. My parents coined the name "Wilma the Whiner," and if ever I let the emotions in my body rise to the surface, they sang it in unison to humiliate me. I learned to mask myself as if my being a well of emotions was something to be ashamed of, something to be sorry for. I didn't want the judgment or the stigma of being too soft to ruin the idea that I was also strong. My parents called it being "too sensitive" and pop-culture psychology refers to it as being an "empath," but I just know it as the way I move through the world. I've always been a feeler. There are a million reasons you might assume why: my trauma, my neurodivergence, or just my humanity. Feeling my feelings openly, loudly, and unapologetically has been both my burden and my superpower. The world needs your softness.

show up for your-
self.

tiny rituals

for shifting & transitions

Put your bare FEET on
the FLOOr to HELP
ground yourself

MAKE DAILY to-do Lists
to KEEP yourSELF
FOCUSED

DriNK WATER

KEEP AN AMETHYST
NEArBY For CALM

tiNY SELF

Inner-child work definitely sounds like some weird, woo-woo stuff; believe me, I *know*. But tending to my inner child has been weird and life-altering healing work. I often think of my small self and hope I can do right by her now. I feel myself crawl under the covers to meet her where she's hiding and let her know it's going to be okay, that she didn't deserve the things that happened to her, and that she will be safe now.

REMINDERS FOR TINY SELF:

YOU ARE SAFE.

YOU ARE LOVED.

WHO YOU ARE IS VALID.

YOU DESERVE FRIENDSHIP.

YOU DESERVE ACCESS TO OPPORTUNITIES.

YOU HAVE A PLACE IN THIS WORLD.

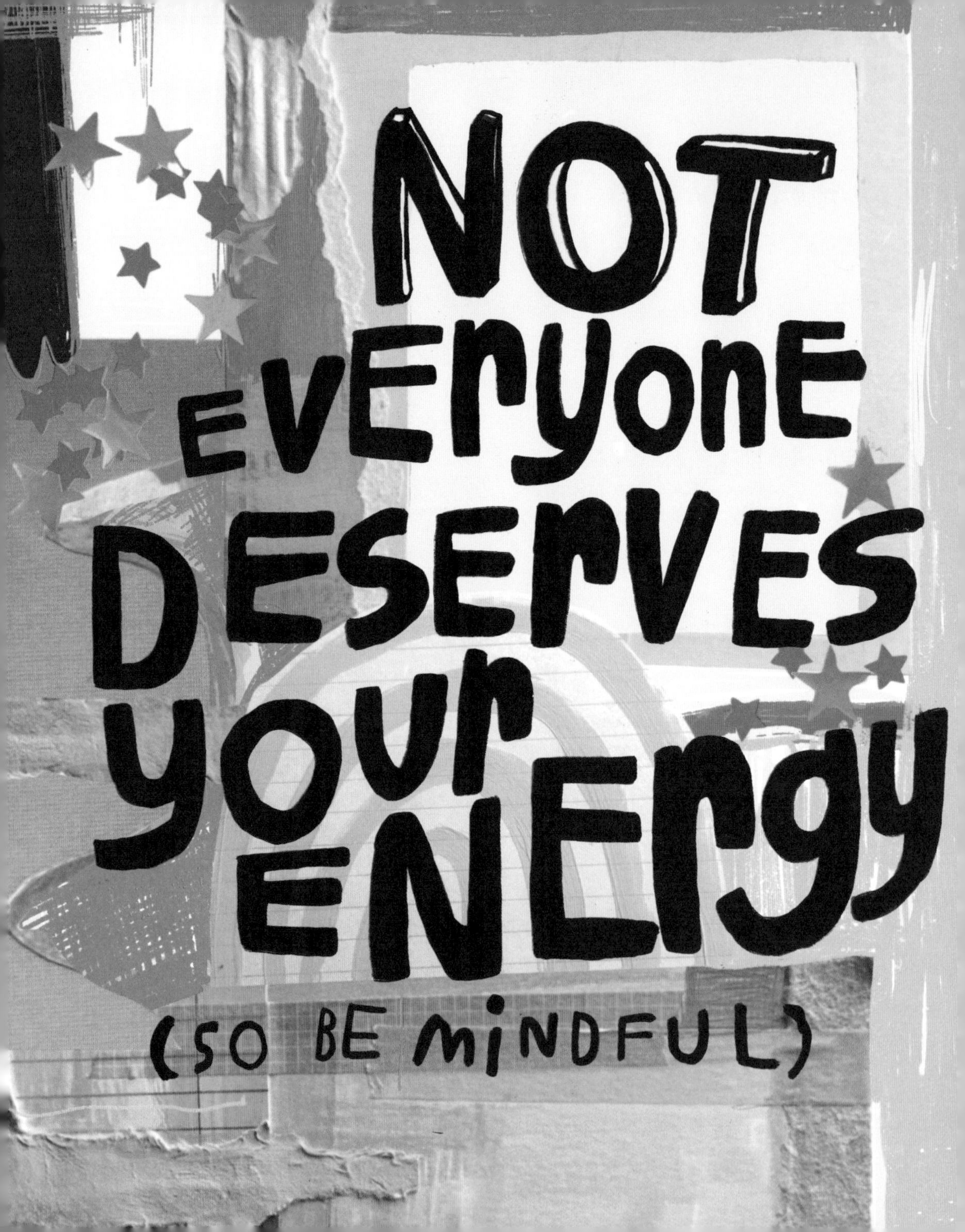
NOT EVERYONE DESERVES YOUR ENERGY
(SO BE MINDFUL)

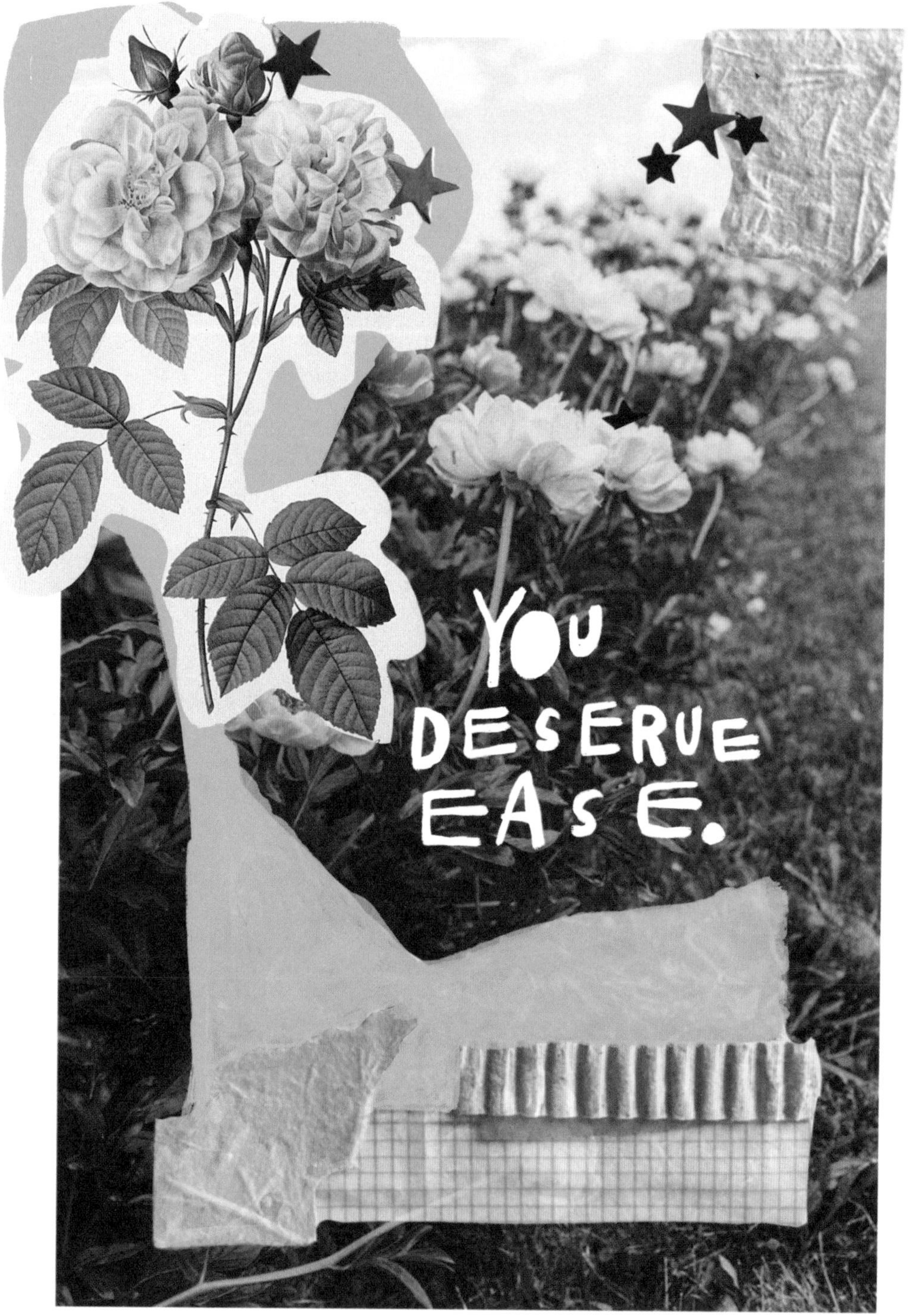
YOU
DESERVE
EASE.

SHAME is A THiEF

Let's talk about shame. Anyone else want to run the minute it's mentioned? It's a word that feels weighty when it leaves your lips. It took me a long time to understand that so much of the discomfort I felt in life was shame. And not just my own shame: society's shame, personal shame, parental shame. I mean, it basically touched every aspect of my life, and I wasn't even sure what it was I was feeling. I've been labeled "depressed" since I was a child; sadness just seemed to be my natural state of being. I didn't really question it or dig deeper; I thought I was just a sad person and that most things in life made me sad, as if it was just my default setting. Over time I've learned that sadness is, for me, usually covering something else. Maybe it's something I don't understand yet, but uprooting the shame attached to the feeling is pivotal.

It sometimes comes in unknowingly, or over time, and redefines how we think of ourselves. We become the shame. We believe we are flawed and incapable of doing things right, and we act in accordance with those beliefs.

SHAME CAN CORRUPT
OUR CALM.

SHAME IS
HEAVVVVY.

SHAME KEEPS US FROM
EXPERIENCING JOY.

SHAME KEEPS US
FROM HEALING.

SHAME KEEPS US
FROM SELF-FORGIVENESS.

SHAME KEEPS US
STUCK.

SHAME KEEPS US
SMALL.

SOME
VERSiONS
OF YOURSELF
WiLL ALWAYS
BE HARD TO FACE

BUT HELP YOU SEE YOUR growth.

give
your-
SELF
grACE.

Because I had so much childhood shame, I took on blame for all things and made them my responsibility to cart from life to life and to be sorry for—and to be punished for, repeatedly and without restraint.

I hurt myself and let other people hurt me, all because the foundational truth in my head was that *I* was broken.

There has been a constant theme of self-sabotage in my life and relationships for as long as I can remember, and I still have to actively fight against falling into it.

What is the antidote to shame? Compassion, self-forgiveness, and letting go.

Own your part of situations, but *only your part*. That's being accountable.

The rest is to be shredded. It's not yours to carry.

If there's one thing I've really come to understand in dismantling and pivoting my life as an adult, it's that shit gets *heavy*. Like, *really* heavy. And life doesn't slow down or stop adding to your load just because your plate is full.

You deserve freedom and you deserve ease.

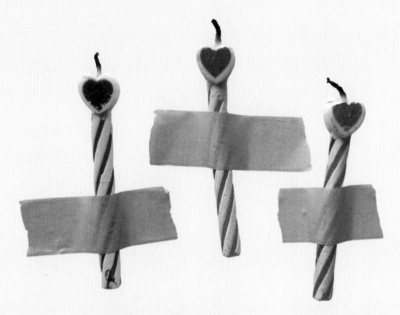

CELEBRATE WHO
YOU ARE
BECOMING.

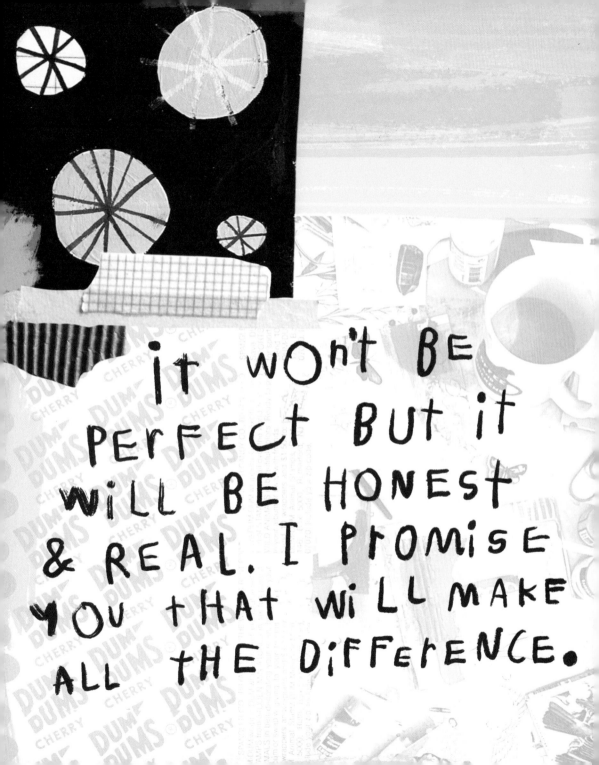

it won't be perfect but it will be honest & real. I promise you that will make all the difference.

minding the MOOn

The year I came out of the closet, I felt so many things fall away from me. I was desperately searching for something to grasp, something to let me know I'd be okay.

I spent most of my twenties inside the delusional grip of organized religion, thinking this was something that would really be there to hold in times of trial. When that wasn't the case, I became really jaded about the idea of God or any spiritual entity, which honestly sucked, because faith was something that had provided me with a good deal of comfort for a good chunk of my life. It was like not reading the fine print on a label: LIMITLESS LOVE IS YOURS! (Unless you are gay, get divorced, have an affair, want to think outside the box, ask questions, or fail to live up to any of these three thousand unattainable ideals that define your worthiness.)

I had to find a new method of finding and learning about myself outside the construct of a bunch of rules some old white men decided were law.

I started collecting crystals because they were pretty and colorful and I could physically hold them when I needed soothing. I would tell people I didn't care if they were a placebo because I felt better having them around. If nothing else, they're pretty to look at and don't hurt anyone, so even though people thought I was going mad, they could all kiss my ass. I became a true "crystal girlie" and honestly loved every minute of it. I brought crystals to my friends' new homes, I had amethyst on every bedside table in our house, and I even had crystals falling out of my sports bra while doing downward dog at yoga. I was always clicking and clanking around, making sure my people and spaces were protected. I used to always say crystals are "hope you can hold," and they really helped me get through some tough times. All of this is to say that healing is hard and figuring yourself out is uncomfortable, and if you need to hold on to something to get through it, I hope you do that. Vibes, crystals, church, gardening, praying, witchery, cooking—let something be your religion. Let there be something to remind you there's a part after this part, and it's worth hanging on for.

NOTE to SELF:

YOU WErE ALWAYs

ENOUGH

HEALING

HAPPENS

IN

LAYERS.

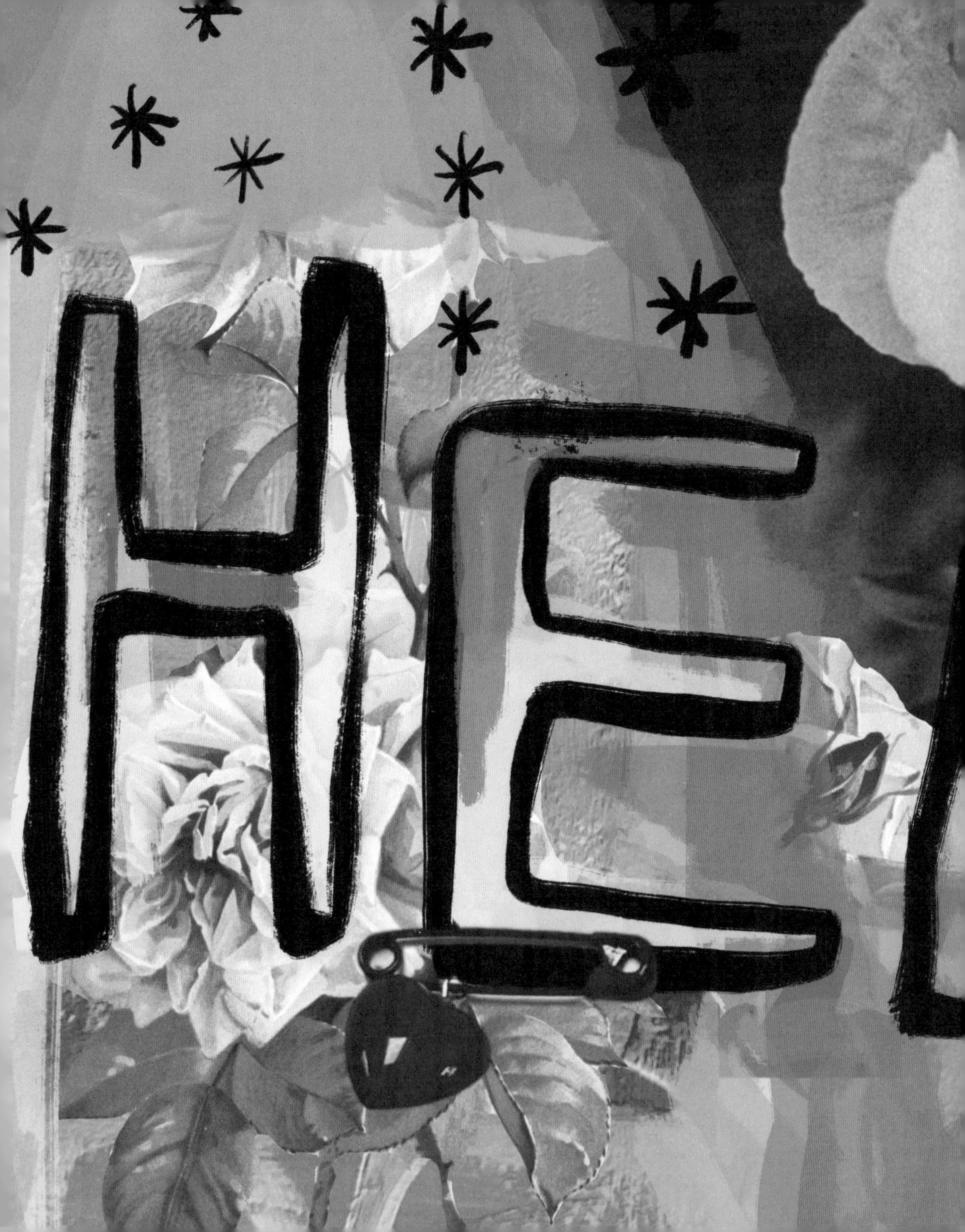
HE

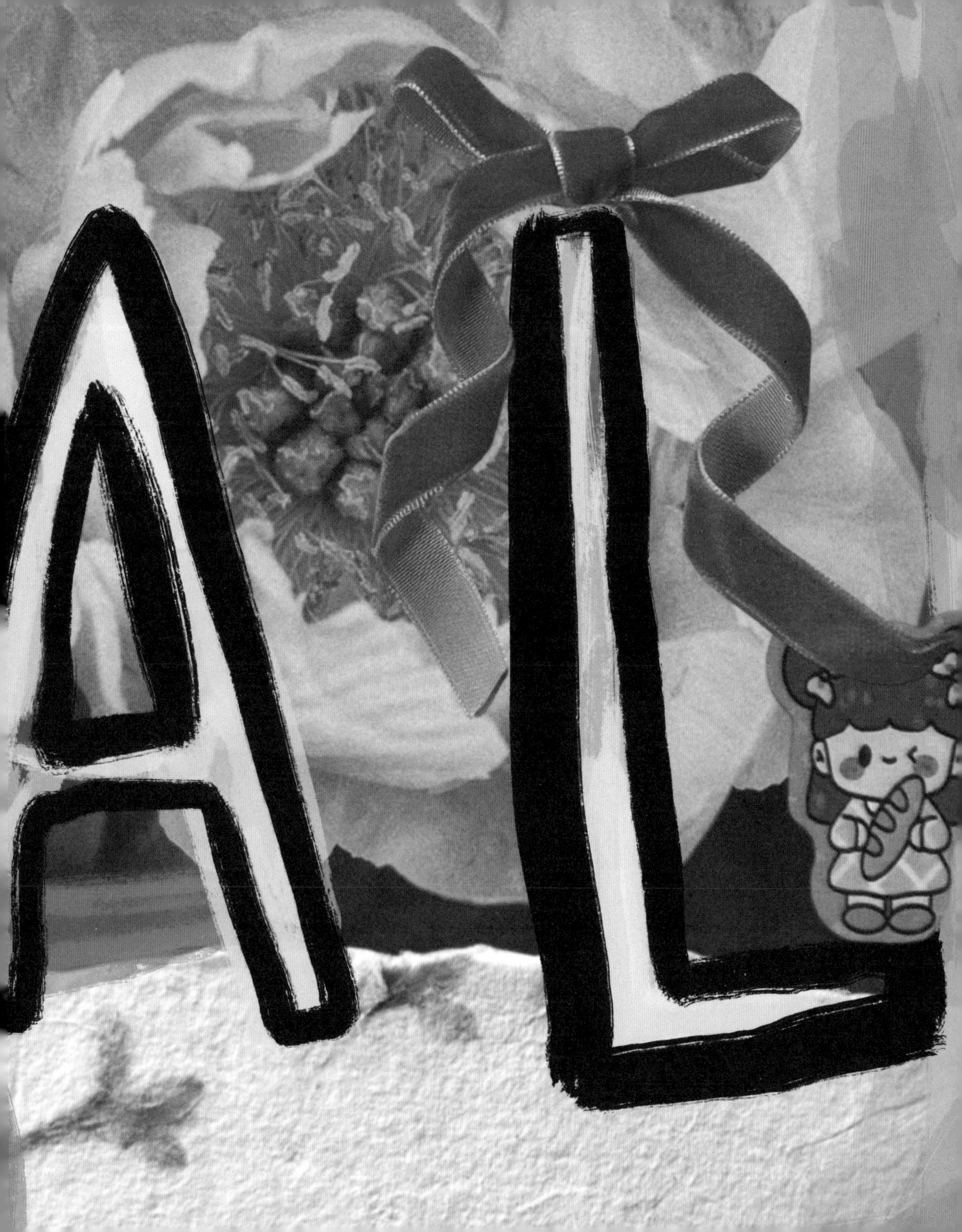
AL

tHE SCArs WE kEEP

I like to keep my trauma in nice, neat boxes.

Call it control, or coping, or whatever, but once I've handled it to the best of my ability, I try to pack it up and stow it away. But when the boxes get bumped, knocked over, or reopened without warning, I'm left feeling pretty wounded.

I can see my own growth because what would once knock me to the floor and leave me in the fetal position for days now just sort of feels like a stomachache. It pangs and bubbles, but I can (for the most part) move through my day. I'm always left wondering why certain things don't heal, or at least why they don't feel like they heal with time.

Why can one text or the sight of someone or a memory bring the feeling back so vividly that it's as if it happened yesterday?

I'm starting to realize that it's because emotional wounds vary in severity just like physical ones. Think of a paper cut: It slices fast and painfully, and usually bleeds. It feels like the worst possible thing in the moment, but when it heals, you forget it was ever there. You don't spend time examining your fingers for old paper cuts. But when you get a wound that leaves a scar, that's something totally different. When I was thirteen, my parents lived a few blocks away from each other, so we would walk or ride our bikes back and forth when we forgot things. One time it was getting dark, and my brother was on foot and I was on my bike. He jumped out of some bushes and scared the shit out of me, and I fell off my bike and scraped my chin across the sidewalk. There was blood everywhere, and I ended up with thirteen stitches in my tiny chin. I wore a Hello Kitty Band-Aid across the bottom of my seventh-grade, mortified middle school face. Now that I'm in my mid-thirties, you can barely see the scar. Almost no one can but me. And I've forgotten so many details I once knew about that moment. I think it's because I put them in a box and moved on, but even though my mind has packed them away and forgotten them, *my body remembers*. So, when I see that scar, I remember the pain, I remember the feelings, and I remember the healing. I think that's what happens with relationship wounds, too. Some heal fully because they didn't cut as deep—but the ones that leave scars the body will always remember, no matter how much we heal or get ourselves into a healthy place. And so, when we're confronted with something that hits the scar, our body feels it even if we mentally feel like we had it taken care of. Give yourself grace. There may be some things you never get over because they left scars, reminders. Some wounds you may have to reopen or reassess to ensure that they've healed as fully as possible. Some pain will wash away, and some will need to be cleaned and cured. You are capable of both types of healing. The grief of something doesn't mean you're not over it or that you never healed from it. It's just a reminder, a scar, a memory.

SOMETIMES WHAT FEELS LIKE AN ENDING is ACTUALLY JUST A NEW BEGINNING.

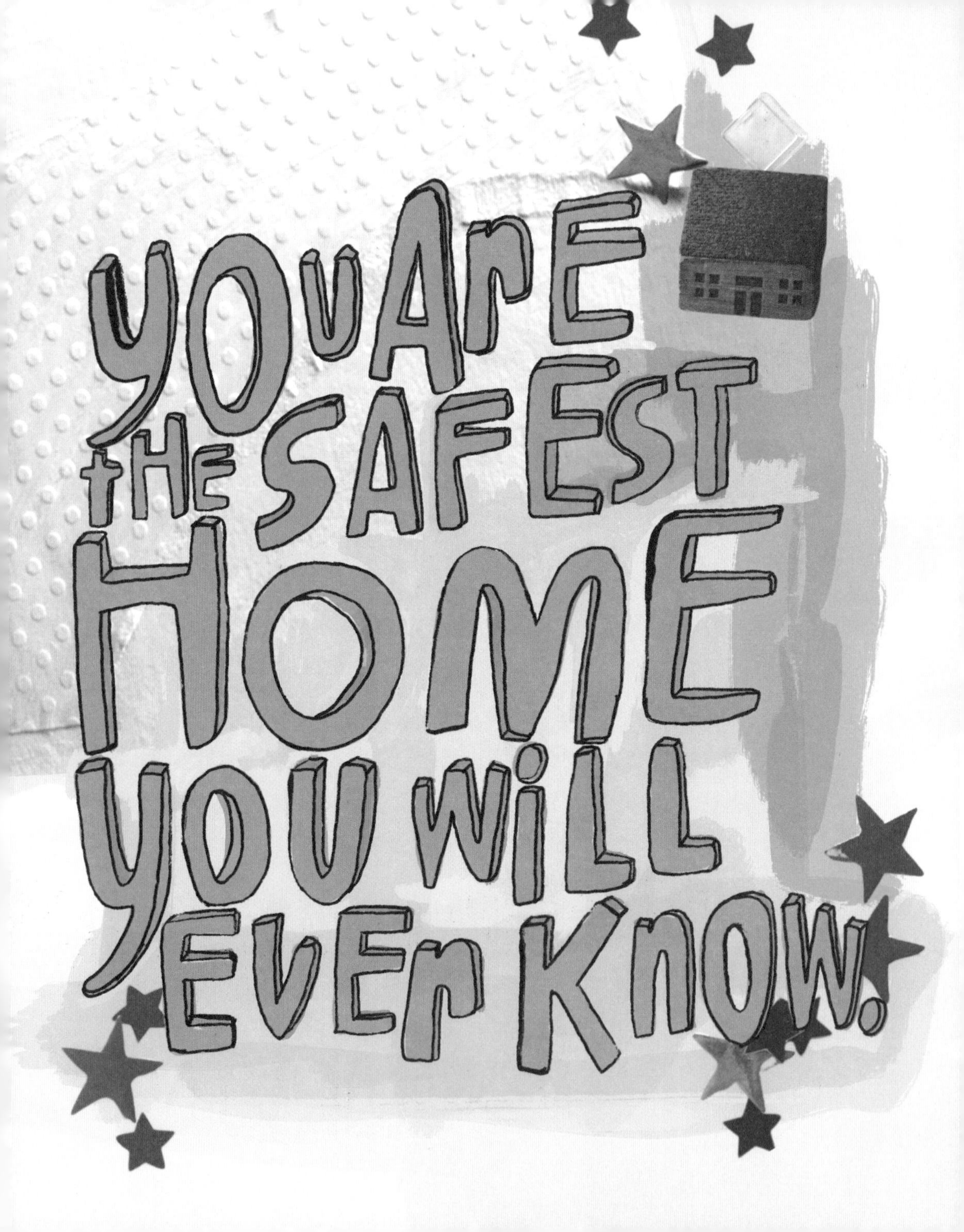
YOU ARE
THE SAFEST
HOME
YOU WILL
EVER KNOW.

YOU ARE HOME

This is a reminder that you are the safest home you will ever have. Take good care of yourself. Make it a nice place to be. Create an environment that's conducive to your personal healing and growth. Hang some plants. Declutter from people, mindsets, and whatever else no longer serves you. Build a fence with two gates—the first to keep out the negativity that may come from others, and the second to open and discard the negativity that may come from your own headspace.

$$\frac{\text{VALUING YOURSELF}}{\substack{\text{VALUING OTHERS'}\\ \text{OPINIONS}}}$$

SOME PEOPLE SUCK & YOUR VALUE IS NOT DETERMINED BY OTHERS.

yOU Are wortH MOre tHAN wHAt PEOPLE tHiNK ABoUT YoU oN tHE iNtErNET

There likely isn't much that hasn't been said about this, but I'm saying it again anyway: Whether five or five hundred thousand people find you in online spaces, please remember that likes and hearts and follows are not real love. You are far more deserving than that. I've been admired and I've been shamed. I've been reposted and shouted out by some of the biggest celebrities, and I've also had hate accounts made about me by former friends and people trying to discredit me. And the thing is that neither matters. What matters is when you close your screen and look in the mirror. Do you know that person is worthy of acceptance? When you exit the apps and look your partner/friend/dog in the face and understand that you are deeply loved and lovable, do you forget what cyberspace thinks of you? I hope so. I hope you invest in that type of love. Likes are fickle and fleeting; self-love is a bottomless well that will refill you for life.

HOW tO BEFriEND YOUr FEAr:

fEAr: friEND or FOE?

When my kids are scared of doing something, I usually ask them what scares them about doing it. We break down the components of their fear. We talk about what's true, what's real, and what's just perceived because we're scared. We take deep breaths, we validate the fear, we give it space to exist, and then we move forward.

Fears aren't entirely bad. Fear can be what keeps children safe. It helps us to assess situations and make informed decisions: not to touch a hot stove, not to run into the road without looking. Fear can be healthy, but sometimes, because of our individual experiences, our fears can be distorted. We can build fear up so high that we cannot see over it. We let it become something we feel is against us instead of something that aids us, that helps us slow down to make sure we're in alignment with ourselves. This happens when our fear becomes the voices around us instead of the voice within us.

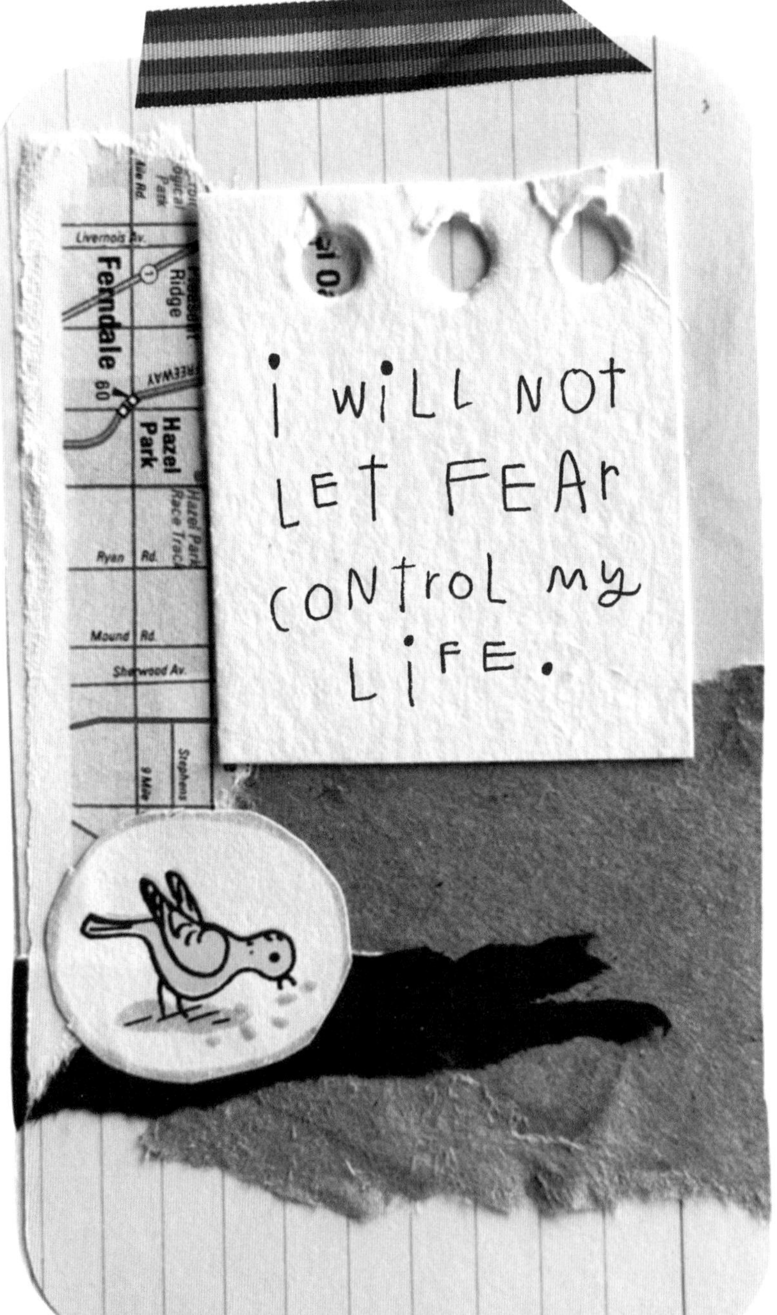
i WiLL NOT
LET FEAr
CONTroL my
LiFE.
Livernois Av.
Ferndale
Ridge
Hazel Park
Ryan Rd.
Mound Rd.
Sherwood Av.

Fear kept me small for most of my life. It took me a long time to realize that most of that apprehension was built on how I thought others might feel and not necessarily how I felt about my fear. The way to hear your own voice in fear is to befriend it. Your fear wants to be heard; it wants space, it wants to be validated, but it's happy to walk alongside you and not stand in your way. The more I could sit with myself and listen to my fear, the more I could acknowledge it and understand it. It takes time and practice. The immediate desire to shut it down and shut it out will come; that's okay. Remember, becoming attuned to your own voice is a practice worth sticking to.

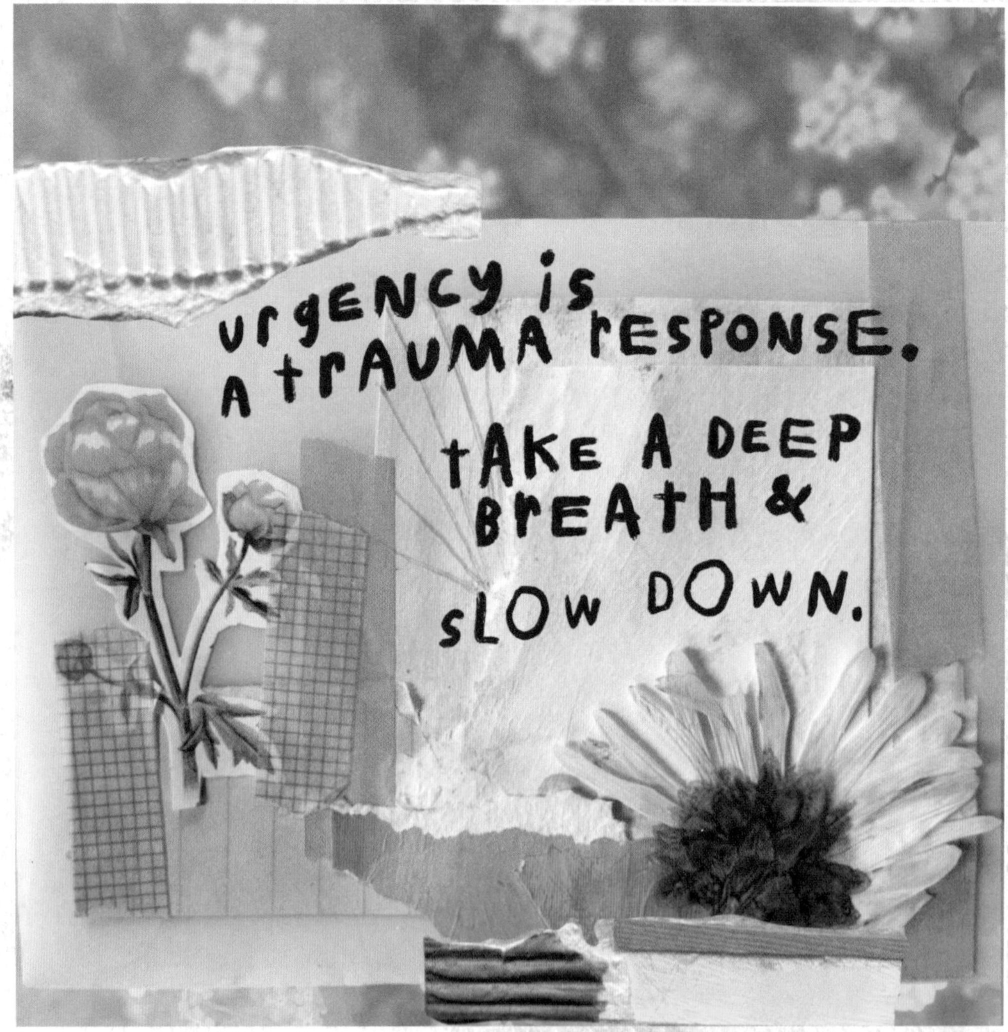
urgency is
a trauma response.
take a deep
breath &
slow down.

shifting through the eras of becoming my truest self.

(it's not easy)

tiny rituAls
FOR GRiEF

LiGHT A CANDLE.

Cry. THEN CRY SOME MORE.

rememBeR it tAKES tiME.

GO OUtSiDE & BreAtHE DEEPLY.

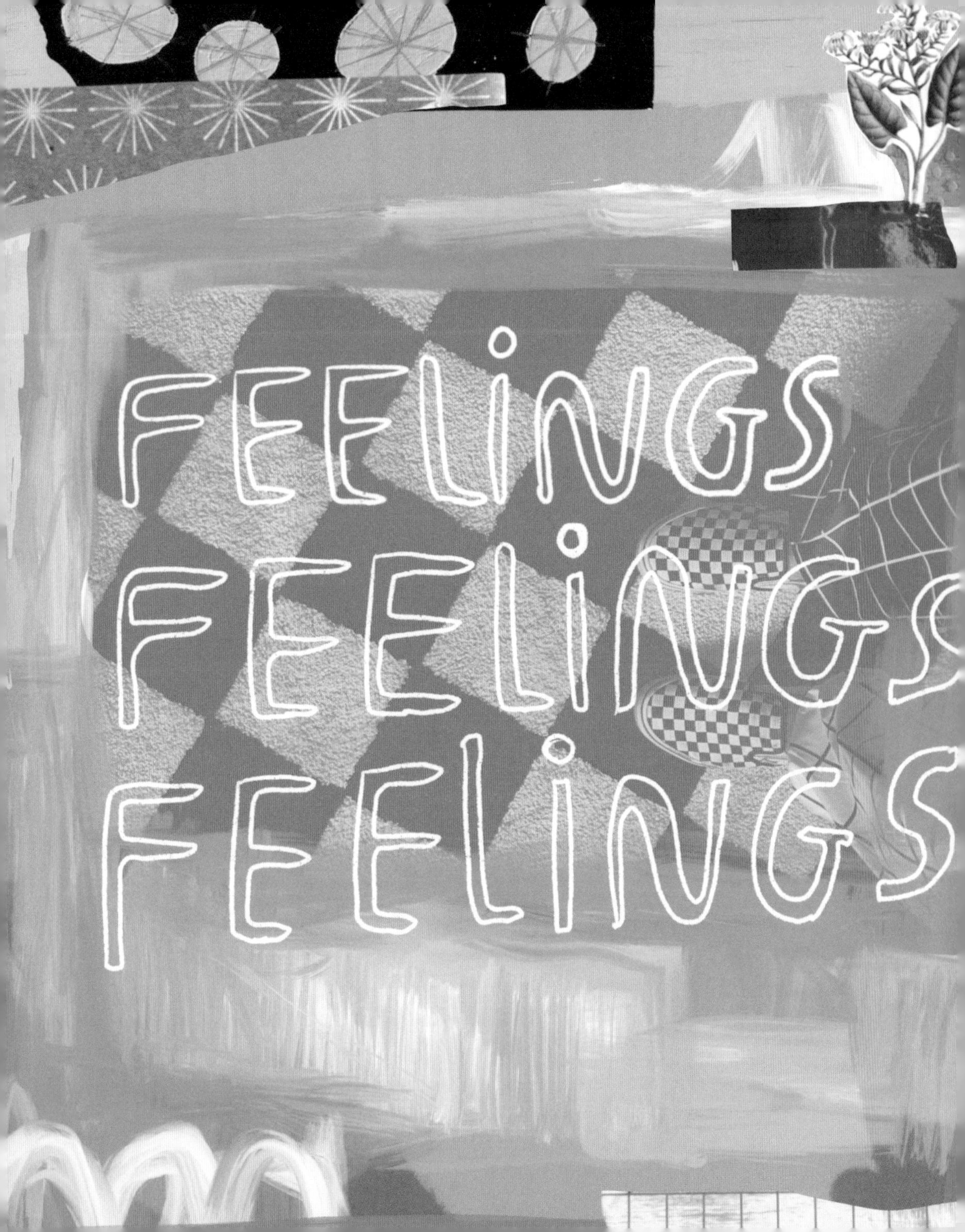
FEELINGS
FEELINGS
FEELINGS

SHAME SHREDDING

Once my therapist asked me to visualize my shame:

"What does your shame physically feel like?"

"I guess it's sort of heavy, like weights or a heavy backpack."

"Okay, but how do you get rid of it?"

"Uhhhh, set it down?"

"Yup! And walk away."

Here I panicked: "*Nooo, I can't!* It's my responsibility. I can't just leave it there for someone else to trip over."

She said, "What do you want to do, bury it and visit it like a shame cemetery? That's not healthy!"

"No, no, I don't want to visit. . . . How about a box? I process it, forgive myself, and then pack it away."

"So it can sit in your attic, collecting dust and cobwebs, and you find it someday and relive the shame you thought you handled? Not again."

"Okay, okay. What if I shred it?"

"Ohhhh! Okay, I like that. It's there but it can't be put back together."

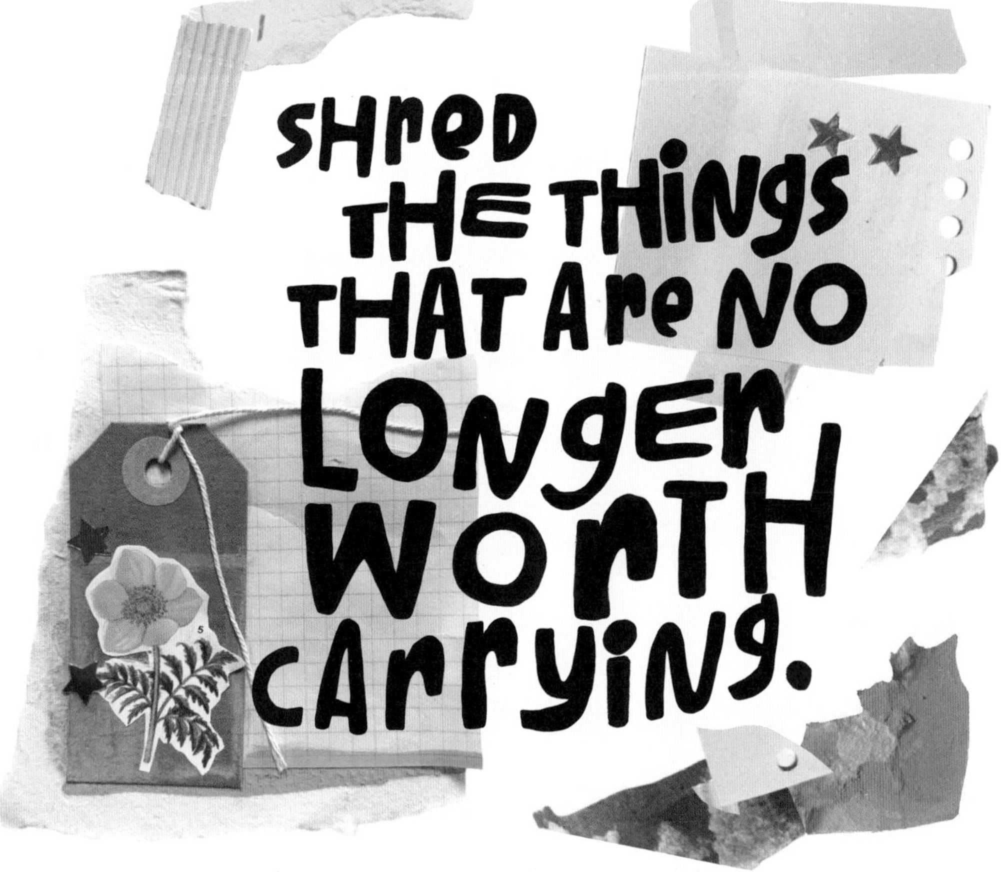
SHRED THE THINGS THAT ARE NO LONGER WORTH CARRYING.

"Or it can be recycled!"

"Oh, yes, you could use it in a new way!"

"Yes! Completely transform it into something else!"

So we created the term *shame shredding*.

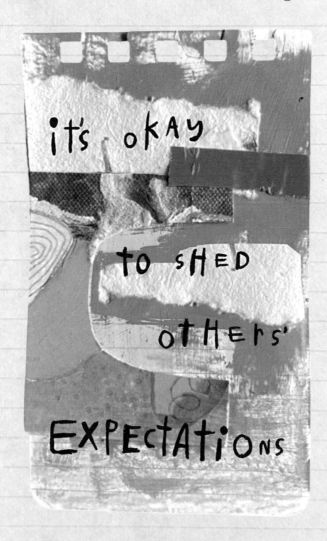

it's oKAY to sHED otHErs' EXPEctATioNs

Doing your Best

I've never set an alarm in my whole life. Between being one of those early to bed, early to rise–type of kids, having babies in my twenties who made their own schedules, and my current stress-induced insomnia that generally leaves me staring at the ceiling until the sun comes up, I've never really needed one. So, when the amount of light peeking through the windows seems about six a.m.–ish, I roll over to verify by checking the time on my phone. Then I begin my descent downstairs as my smooshed-face pug gleefully bites at my house shoes in hopes that I will move faster to the back door. I push the glass slider with two hands because I accidentally broke the handle off three months ago and it's now on the ever-running list of projects I plan to get to. Our pup, Frankie, excitedly leaps outside and looks back to me at the top of the deck stairs because she is as needy as everyone else in my house and cannot pee without my presence, so I step outside in my boxers and hole-y

T-shirt that I refuse to throw away because it's the perfect amount of worn and breathe in the crisp morning air. This process is the same whether it's 70 degrees or 12, the only difference being that I might switch my house shoes for boots if needed because I'm way too lazy to run back up the stairs to put something more weather appropriate on. By the time Frankie finally finds a spot in the backyard that she deems acceptable to pee in, I must run inside to relieve myself, because I've had two babies and my pelvic floor is about as strong as my teenage will to live. I dump yesterday's unfinished coffee into our white porcelain double-basin farmhouse sink and watch as it trickles like a fountain down all the dishes I should have loaded into the dishwasher the night before. If it's a day I have my kiddos, I start to make their lunches, clean out school folders, yell up the stairs to remind them that getting dressed for the day means clean underwear, and beckon twenty times or so to get their shoes and coats on so I can drop them off. If I don't have the kids, the routine is the same, except instead of school prepping, I spend that hour loading those dishes and maybe vacuuming or mopping up the accident Frankie left me on the hardwood floor because I laid in bed for two extra minutes and she's a spiteful princess.

I then usually decide it's time to be productive. I walk back up two flights of stairs (embarrassed by how much my legs hurt) to our finished attic. I moved my studio both to save money and because I thought it would help my focus and streamline my chaotic brain. I usually light incense and my altar candles and put on either my sad-girl music or Cardi B, because it really depends on which one of my personalities is driving the bus that day. I would love to be one of those creatives who immediately sits down and dives into their well of inspiration with enough extra mental space to create one or seven social media posts, but instead I usually decide that my physical space is too messy to create in and spend the first one to five hours sorting, cleaning, and organizing. I've convinced myself that once my space is tidy, the words or art will flow out of me so easily that it won't even feel like work. But somewhere along the way my neurodivergent ass gets sucked into a spiral of nostalgia, reminiscing, and falling into feelings, or I get hyperfixated on creating visually pleasing labels for my freshly sorted materials with my vintage hand punch label maker that does wonders for my carpel tunnel, but who cares because ~*aEsTHetiCs*~. I realize it's almost lunchtime and sink into my fear of wasting the day without accomplishing any of the things I needed to accomplish while also contemplating whether I should eat and trying to figure out if my anxiety is from forgetting my meds or drinking too much coffee or maybe a combination of both.

This is my routine, and it varies daily based on so many things. Did I get enough sleep? How many times did my children come into the room? Sometimes I feel like a total waste of atoms, and some days I feel like I'm contributing to the world in a beautiful and special way. But the one thing that's always consistent is that I wake up. That's one thing I can say I've done every day of my thirty-five years of life. Be it depressed, joyful, heartbroken, inspired, uneasy, sleepy, or meh, I open my eyes and I try. None of us are ever going to be able to show up 100 percent every day. Not even when we're healing. Not even when we're taking meds. Not even when we're in therapy. Not even when we're living authentic, expansive, magical lives. There will always be days when we would rather stay inside under the blankets and cry. There will always be days when the TV judges us by asking if we're still watching when we know we have a deadline for school or work and are pretending it doesn't exist. There will always be days when we do everything we can and still feel like we're falling short. That's just being human. Sometimes I do my meal prep and finish the laundry, play outside with my kids, and give my partner quality attention; doing my best might look different each day. If we wake up and show up in whatever capacity we can, we're already overcomers.

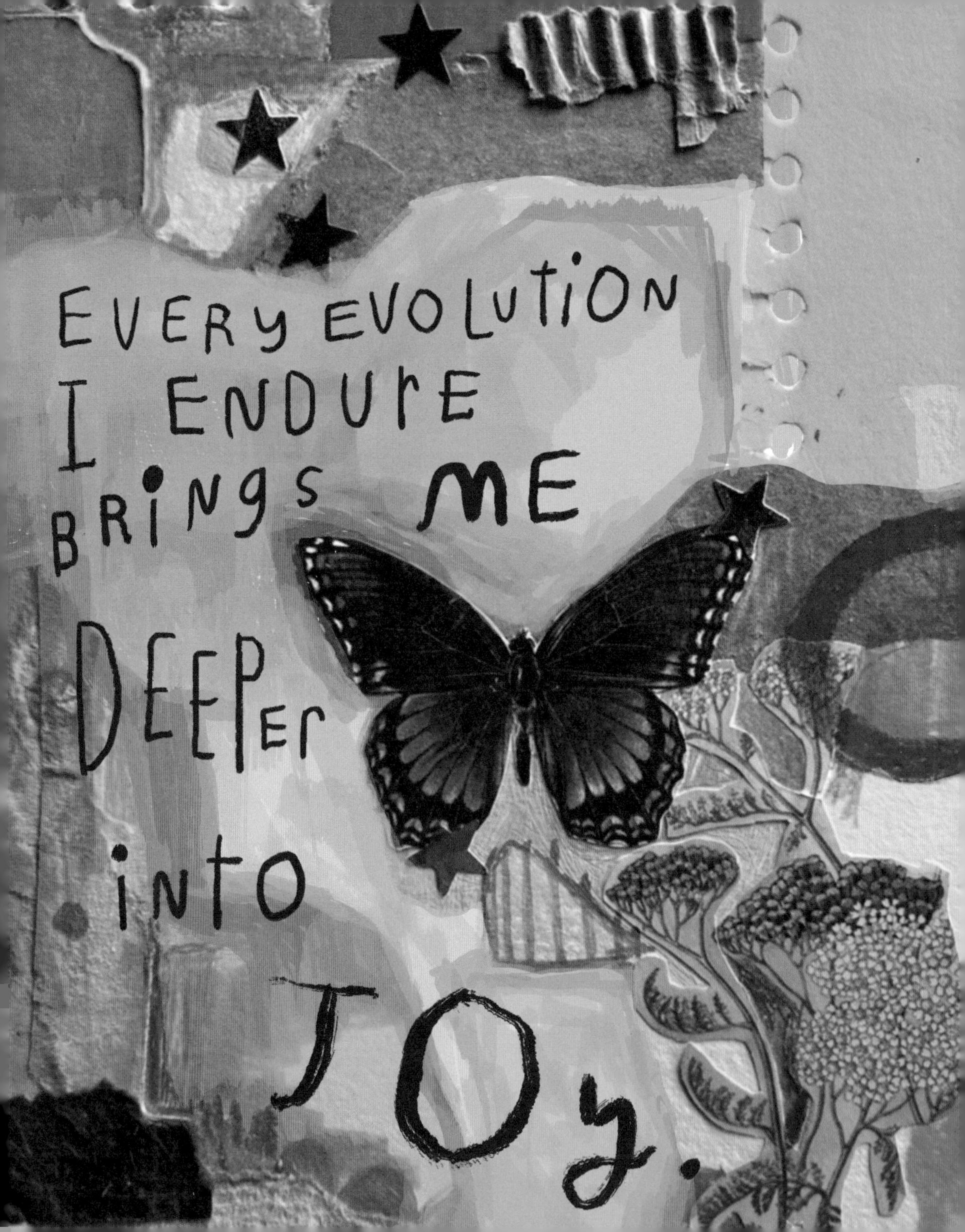
EVERY EVOLUTION
I ENDUrE
BRiNgS ME
DEEPEr
iNTO
JOy.

self-love is a radical act in a world that's trying to keep us small.

SELF-trust
LOOKS LiKE:

SPEAKING to yOURSELF
WITH KiNDNESS

SETTING BOUNDAriES
& KEEPING THEM

VALiDATiNG yOUr OWN
EMOTiONS

KNOWiNG MistAKES HAPPEN
& BEiNG ABLE to LET THEM GO

trusting your ABiLity to
MAKE DECisiONS

Practicing SELF-LOVE

rEALizing AND Acting
iN ACCOrDANCE WiTH
yOUr VALUES

HoW I LEArNED to trust mySELF

Maya Angelou said, "I learned a long time ago the wisest thing I can do is be on my own side." It unfortunately took me much longer to learn this lesson. If I didn't know how to love myself, I most certainly didn't know how to trust myself. I didn't know how to be on my own side. I didn't even know I had a side worth protecting. How would I even begin to do that when my concept of reality was constantly questioned and invalidated in childhood? I was criticized so much that I kept shrinking to keep myself safe, quieting the gnawing I would sometimes feel inside for fear of being wrong. I would self-abandon over and over, telling myself I wasn't smart enough, wasn't good enough, wasn't nearly what was needed. I would seek everyone's opinion before I made any decisions, feeling there was no way I could make the "right" decision on my own. I needed people to weigh in, to give me insight into myself. Do you know

how crazy that sounds? Even as I type it, I shake my head at the past me. I feel for them. Who is going to know me better than me? How will the people around me know what will make me happy, or balanced, or not have regret? They won't. They won't know my boundaries, or what will make me happy, or how to express my feelings for myself.

You have to do that: you have to be your biggest advocate and cheerleader, the one still cheering when maybe no one else is, when it feels like there's no one in your corner. Take a deep breath and know that you can and will handle this. Sometimes change is an invitation to self-trust.

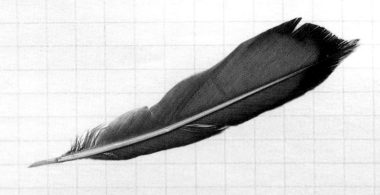

tiny rituALs
FOR LOving
Yourself

stretch your BODY

DRINK COFFEE WiTH CREAM

HANG HANDWRiTTEN AFFiRMATiONS
NExt to YOUR MiRROR

GO FOR A WALK

SPEAK KiNDLy tO Yourself

HEALING > HEALED

For those undoing their need to do things "the right way," you'll be heartbroken to know there is no trophy or medal or ribbon in healing. Even worse, you are never simply *done* healing. Healing is a state of being. I think many people say, *All right, I'll go to therapy, get healed, and then start (or restart) my life.* But healing is a process that takes the entirety of your existence as a human. It might not always feel as big and heavy as it does sometimes, but embracing your path is part of making peace with it. Knowing that your healing will ebb and flow and evolve with you is part of what makes healing worth it. You get to take it with you. You get to take the things you learn and the ways you grow into new situations and relationships. You get do-overs and

apologies; you get to relearn and restart. The only right way to heal is to start—to say this shit isn't working and there must be another way. You deserve that. You deserve a calm nervous system. You deserve to have your feelings, no matter how big and overwhelming, and to know that they are simply passing through. You deserve to learn strength for the times you didn't have it in the past and the times you'll need it in the future. You deserve forgiveness—for yourself and for the people who may have hurt you. Embrace your healing with open arms. Throw away your timelines and schedules and heal yourself through what was and what is to come. I really want that for you.

DON'T LET
PAST WOUNDS
KEEP YOU FROM
A WHOLE
FUTURE
FILLED
WITH
JOY

WHAT is JOY?

I think people often confuse joy and happiness. Happiness is a
feeling, but I believe it to be fleeting. It arrives and then passes,
like all our emotions. Joy is different. Joy is a way of being. Joy
is felt throughout your body and mind. Joy is never lost.

CHOSEN FAMILY

Families are wildly complex ecosystems. The word *family* itself used to feel like a weight around my neck, a reminder of yet another reason I felt less than. The image of the nuclear family was one I grew up seeing everywhere. From sitcoms on TV to what high school health class taught were the components of a family, I saw repeatedly that I didn't have a family in any traditional sense. For years I would break my own boundaries and push the limits of my mental health to try to achieve any sense that I had a "good" family. I put myself in uncomfortable situations, taking on things a child should never take on, to try to win the love and reassurance of people who should have been my caregivers. At some point I had to learn that I shouldn't be regularly harmed by someone just because we shared a bloodline. I mourned. I still mourn sometimes for those moments I'll never have with people I'll never really know and who will never really know me.

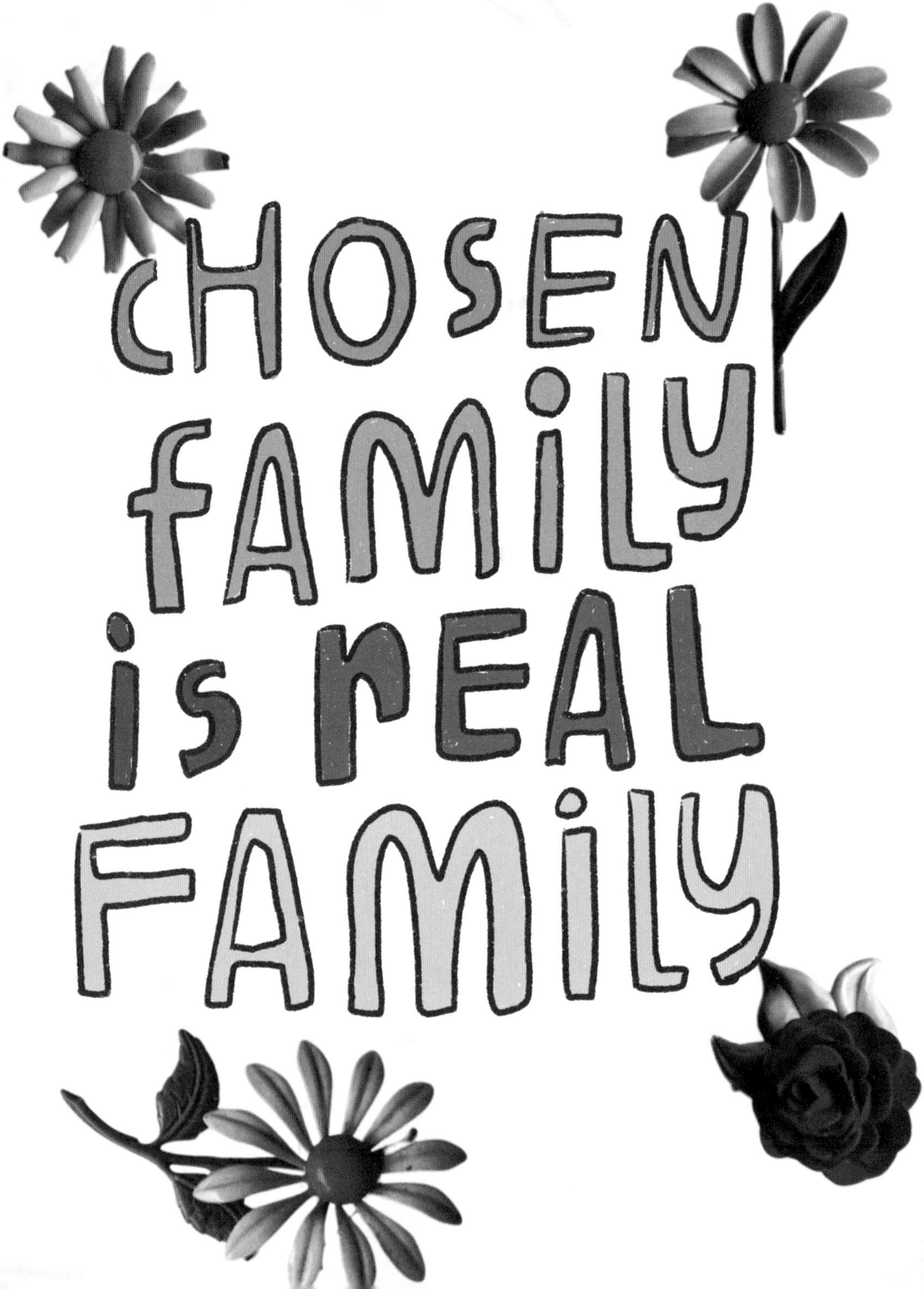
CHOSEN
family
is real
family

The people I share them with may not share my DNA, but they surely share my values, my ethics, my beliefs, and even my humor. *Friend* never felt like enough of a word to truly embody the deep affection, adoration, and kinship I felt for these people. They are my chosen family—which, honestly, I think is way cooler and more meaningful anyway. They aren't tethered to me simply because we have some matching chromosomes but because they were chosen with care based on their actions. They lead with love, and love with respect. There is no obligation, there is no need to cross boundaries, because we all see boundaries as healthy parts of being in a community with each other. I used to let society get in my head and question the validity of this sort of family. But I see so clearly now that there is no comparison. There is no need to investigate or dissect the ones I call family because their motives are clear. They choose to be here. They choose to build families that don't need to fit in a box. They help me build my family based on mutual love. So whatever your family looks like, know that it is precious. However the puzzle pieces of your people fit together, know that you're making a way for future families to see themselves, too.

cOmmUNity KEEPs yOU

Normalize platonic intimacy.

Kiss your friends on the face.

Hold their hand.

Don't suppress the desire to tell them you love them.

Don't reserve the deep well of love you have because of the lie that you have a limited or finite amount that should be given only to the person you are romantically involved with.

Stop believing that the word *intimacy* is synonymous with sex. Intimacy is closeness, intimacy is vulnerability, intimacy is being real.

You deserve connection on a multitude of levels. Don't let others who fear closeness keep you from experiencing intimacy in all its limitless facets.

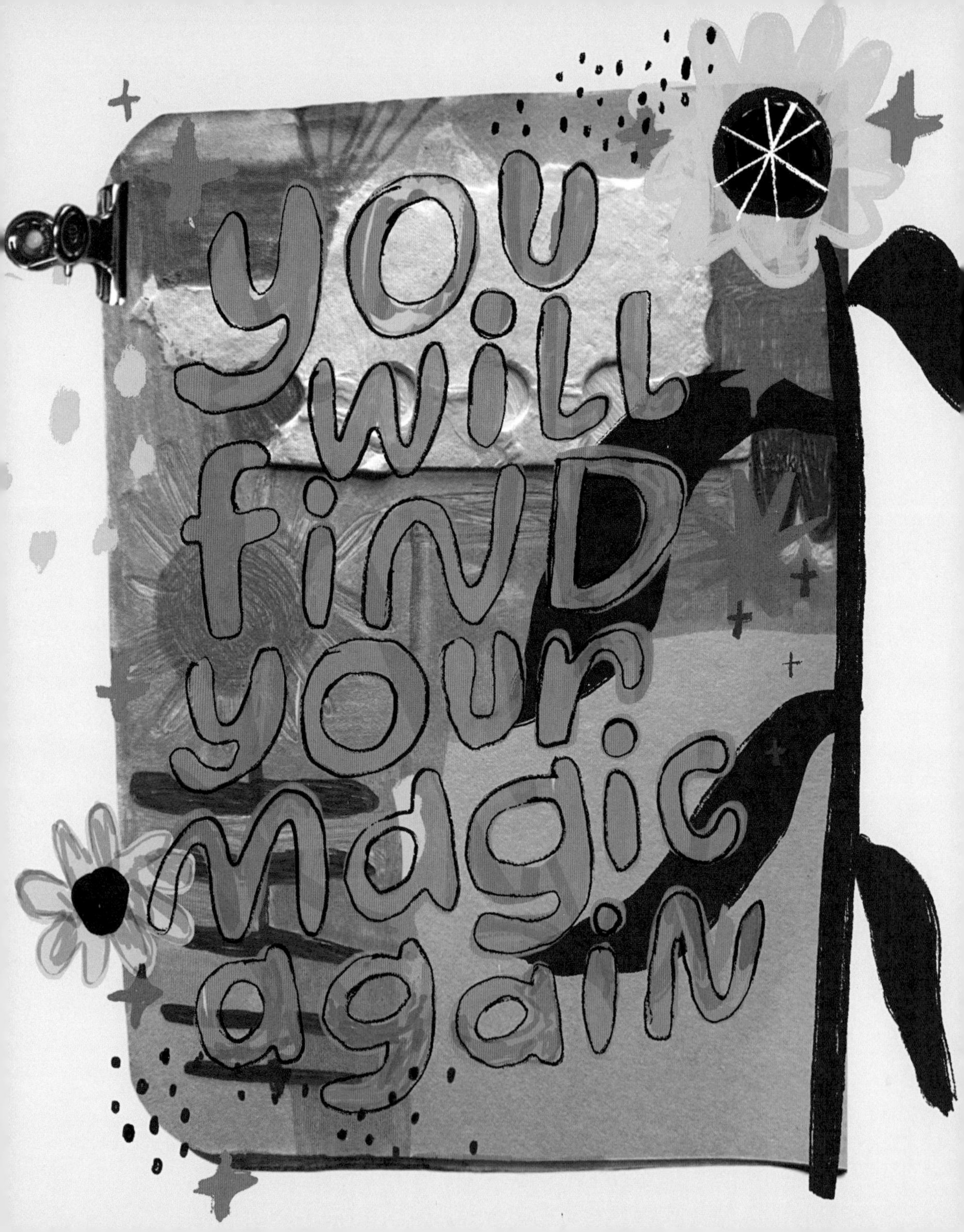
you will find your magic again

tHE MaGic

The process of becoming is where all the messy, painful, evolutionary growth stuff happens.

A line in an Andrea Gibson poem reads, "The sun said, 'It hurts to become,'" and that shit has been ringing through my mind since the day I read it. Metaphorizing is so painful. It requires energy and surrender. It's a reason I relate so strongly to butterflies and moths: there's just something about a fuzzy-worm-thing becoming something completely different and majestic after being wrapped in a pod, something undeniable about everything it goes through to evolve. Something about how it's pure nature to change and not stay the same. These tender parts of becoming are usually where the magic lies.

EMBRACE yOur PROCESS.

THE MAGIC

crying is part of how we HEAL.

crying is COOL

One day in the car, my nine-year-old looked at me and asked, "Mom, are you crying?"

I said, "Yes, honey, I'm just having some big, heavy feelings."

"Some sad feelings?"

"Mm-hmm." I got out while another tear escaped from the uncooperative corners of my eyes.

My kid continued the conversation: "You know what? Sometimes I like crying because I actually feel better after. I'll be angry or sad and almost feel like I can't breathe; then I'll cry and get it all out. I feel so much better. It's like all my sad or angry thoughts go inside each tear, and when they fall out of my eyes, they fall out of my mind. That's why I think crying is good for you: it gets rid of all the sad thoughts in your head."

Crying is cathartic, it's healing, and it's . . . normal. There is no power in denying yourself a completely human response to an overwhelming emotion. It doesn't make you stronger or more resilient; it likely harms you. True courage is knowing that expressing your emotions is a pathway to feeling and processing them. Let the feelings climb into your tears and take the train to the space outside your body. Let your tears soothe you. You don't have to hold it all together all the time. Your body was made for this; it will thank you for giving it what it needs. Crying is cool, so grab some tissues and drink some water, because we all deserve to feel lighter in our pain.

grow

GROW

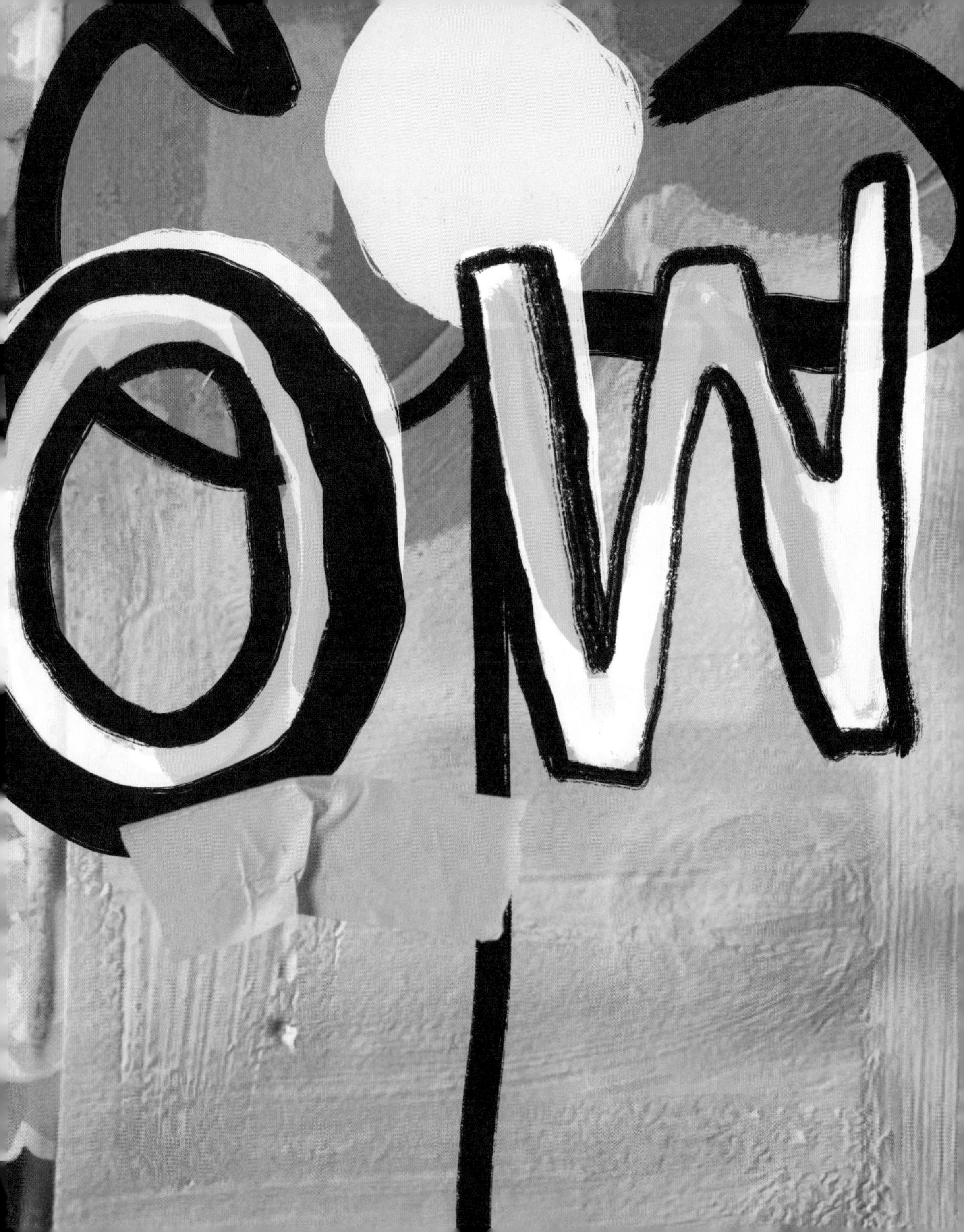
OW

LiViNG witHOut ESCAPE PLANs

Something happened to me in the midst of writing this book. Well, let's be honest about it: a lot of things happened. A second divorce, a suicide attempt, a partial hospitalization program, a pushed-back book deadline, the unearthing of everything I thought I knew and everything I had yet to learn, rebuilding community, learning healthy coping mechanisms, a second coming out, along with, ya know, the regular life of running a business, a community space, trying to raise emotionally intelligent tiny humans, navigating coparenting, and, like, sleeping.

But also somewhere in the swirling chaos of life I stopped living with escape plans. My mother always made me deeply aware that there were ways out of this life, whether they be numbing the hell out of myself, self-harming, running away, or even death. It seemed smart to always have an escape plan ready in case shit got hard. My mom made many attempts on her life while I was growing up, some very traumatic for me as a kid and some I was told about in passing like she'd gone away for a long weekend. It became normal to me and my siblings. I have a lot of memories of visiting her in different facilities with varying levels of care. These experiences became embedded in my being. It was the way we were taught to cope when things got hard. I remember that, for a long time, I kept all my old prescriptions hidden under my clothes in a dresser drawer. I even went as far as to have my brother and sister give me their failed medications under the guise of being responsible, as if I would dispose of them so *they* would be safe and not be tempted to self-harm. But instead I added them to my collection. It's alarming to me now how much comfort I felt in knowing I possessed a small pharmacy beneath my worn-out band tees in the second drawer of my dresser. It was my "just in case"; it was my escape plan if it all got to be too much and I needed to bail.

The most recent attempt was a scream for help. It was a combination of my needing to make everyone happy no matter the cost to myself and feeling like no one was listening. It was my asking for time and space to figure it out and to not feel shamed or rushed or judged in the process. But because my pleas for understanding seemed to go unheard, I reached for my numbing; I reached for the escape plan. When I think back, I didn't even really want to die; I think I just wanted to sleep. I wanted the weight of everything I carried not to fall on me. I wanted to breathe without having to tell myself to breathe.

After I came home, I saw the reality of the wake of that wave. It was gut-wrenching. I made an active decision that I no longer wanted an escape plan for life. I no longer wanted to lean on an "out." After so much sitting with myself, I felt this resolve within me to choose to stop surviving and instead to live. I know that probably sounds ridiculous to make that sort of declaration to yourself, but I needed to. I had lived in survival mode for thirty-five years. Thirty-five years of just doing what it took to get to the next day. I don't know what it's like to live a life—to *really* live it. To not allow the highs and lows of the human experience to sway me in my decision to continue with it.

I think my mind shift from surviving to living helped me make other realizations, too. We talk about our healing journey like it's something we're doing to be able to handle our trauma. But our suffering can become our comfort zone. We heal to live a life that no longer centers on our pain. I think that's what I'm finding real freedom to be. I used to think not having nightmares or flashbacks or constant triggers meant that I had attained some sort of full recovery. But living is not the absence of those things, it's the ability to see life past them.

You aren't supposed to work on healing just so you can handle your trauma; you're supposed to heal so you can experience joy. Joy is inarguably part of my new plan to live. There is no joy in survival, but there *is* joy in really and truly living life. Part of learning this has been separating my identity from my past, from my trauma. I am not my past; my past happened *to* me. It's an important distinction to make to help free you from carrying your pain around forever. Even the things you played a part in: you do not deserve to be tied to them forever. Self-forgiveness is healing.

And that's something I'm beginning to understand.

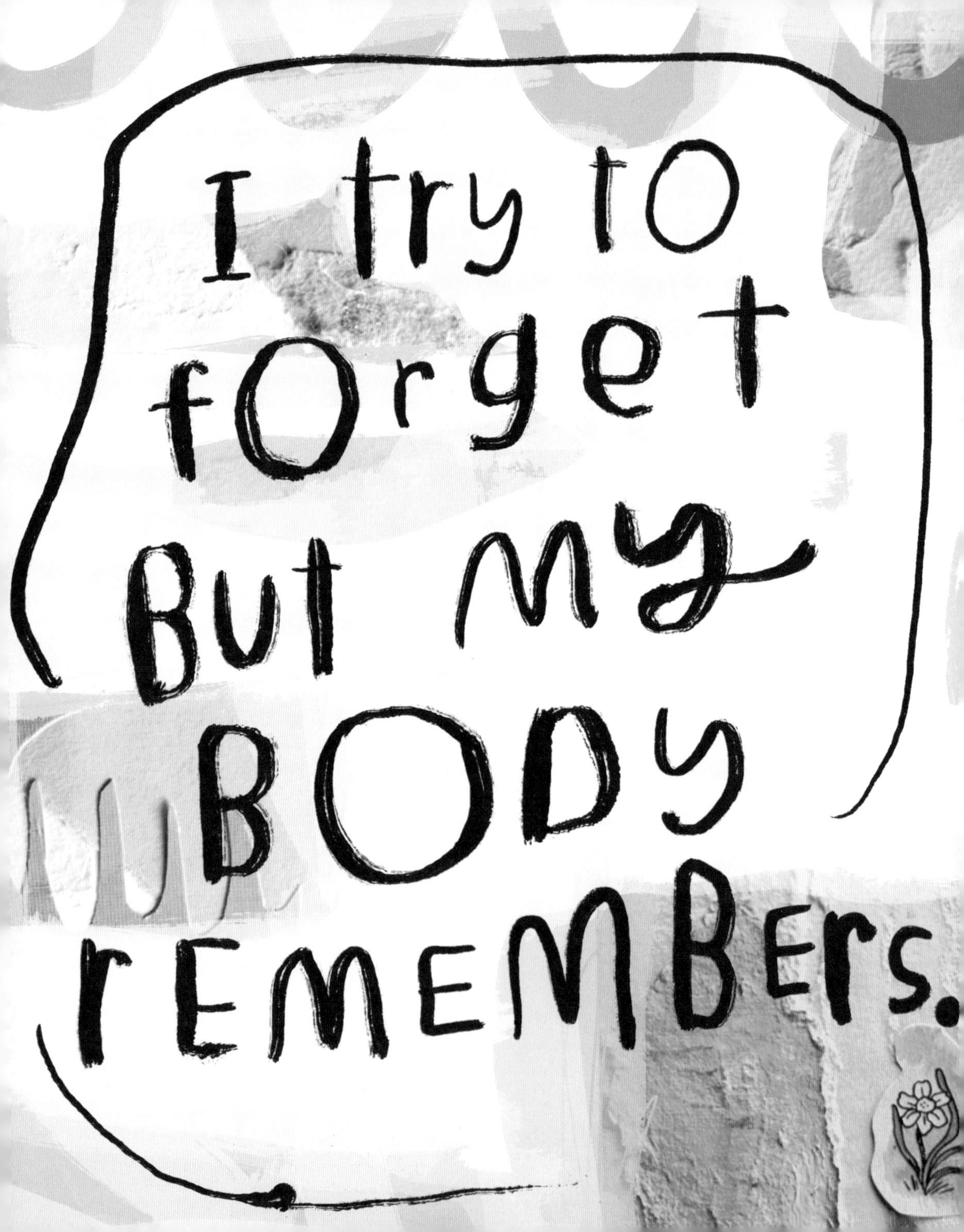
I try to forget but my BODY remembers.

BODY KEEPS THE SCORE

Bodies are weird. I often feel like my body is just some shell or meat suit I wear until I die. I honestly haven't ever invested much in my physical body. I've been hyper-focused for most of my life on who I am as a person: my insides, my feelings, soul stuff. As I get older, I'm starting to value this body of mine—all it holds and all it teaches me. Have you ever had a visceral reaction to something? You may not even want to react or feel the feelings, but your body remembers: your body takes over and feels what it needs to feel. Your body protects and holds you.

Drink More Water
(Yes, I'm Serious)

I don't have all the answers; I maybe actually have none. But something I do know is that I've never heard a bad idea start with "First, let's get some water." Call me crazy, but sometimes I think our minds are spinning so fast, we're so overwhelmed, we're so busy that we forget to tend to what is literally one of our most basic needs: water. Drink some water; drink a bunch of water. Take care of yourself in the most simplistic, life-giving ways. If our most fundamental needs aren't met, how can we assume we'll think clearly and cohesively when making decisions?

I love coffee. Coffee is my comfort. So, over the years, I got accustomed to habitually drinking coffee. If I was bored, or inspired, or lonely, or contemplative, I would reach for a mug and pour the coffee. All. Day. Long. I eventually realized that my comfort coffee was causing me discomfort. I was constantly anxious, never sleeping, hardly eating . . . the list goes on. I decided that, if and when I felt that itch, that craving, to have something to hold, I would go and get some water. Hear me out: I'm not dumb; I know water is not coffee. But I do think that by habitually drinking water and focusing on meeting one of my body's most important requirements, it makes it easier for me to feel more grounded in my ability to breathe and move throughout my day.

So get yourself some cute glasses, a water bottle—hell, even some lemons. Whatever might entice you to stick with a new routine.

Ways to Protect your Peace

Protect your Boundaries

The people who are most upset when you make boundaries are the people who generally benefit from your having none. Most people visualize boundaries as walls, and I think that's what makes others feel like you're just shutting them out or maybe even hiding. But boundaries are doors—the doors to our relationships. All different relationships: people, money, partners, family, friends, even our belongings. They can be opened. You can invite people in. These doors let people know what behavior is tolerated and welcomed in your space, and what behavior would cause you to shut and lock the door. If respected, the door can always be reopened. Walls keep people out; doors keep you in control of your space.

LET PEOPLE BE wrong ABOUT YOU

This is hard to do. I think it's natural to want to defend yourself and your character, but there will be people who are committed to misunderstanding you for their own purposes. Sometimes our ability to let go of the need to combat external noise is where we will find our peace.

BE MINDFUL OF WHO HAS ACCESS TO YOU

Have you ever heard the term *energy vampires*? Learn to recognize them, and don't let them take up too much of your emotional and mental space.

ACCOUNTABILITY

Some versions of yourself will always be painful to face. Shame and regret can sometimes keep us from accepting our part in things. Taking responsibility will set you free. Owning your part in the way things played out will make space for authentic healing.

i FEEL SAD FOR ANYONE i HURT ON MY WAY to UNDERSTANDING MYSELF. SOMETIMES PEOPLE DESERVED BETTER THAN THE PERSON i SHOWED UP AS.

FORgiving yOURSELF iS ESSENTiAL tO yOUR HEALiNG.

NOTes On HEALing

Forgive yourself and forgive
yourself again. Understanding
that you are human is a crucial
part of healing. Making peace with
ourselves and accepting our past
is the only way we will live full,
genuine lives.

HARD PILLS TO SWALLOW:

- SOMETIMES THE ONLY CLOSURE YOU GET IS WITHIN YOURSELF

- SOME PEOPLE WILL NEVER LOVE YOU THE WAY YOU WANT THEM TO

- YOU CANNOT CONTROL OTHERS' REACTIONS

- PEOPLE-PLEASING ONLY HURTS YOU IN THE END

- UNLEARNING YOUR OWN TOXIC SHIT IS HARD, BUT PATTERNS CAN CHANGE

EVERYONE'S GROWTH
LOOKS DIFFERENT.

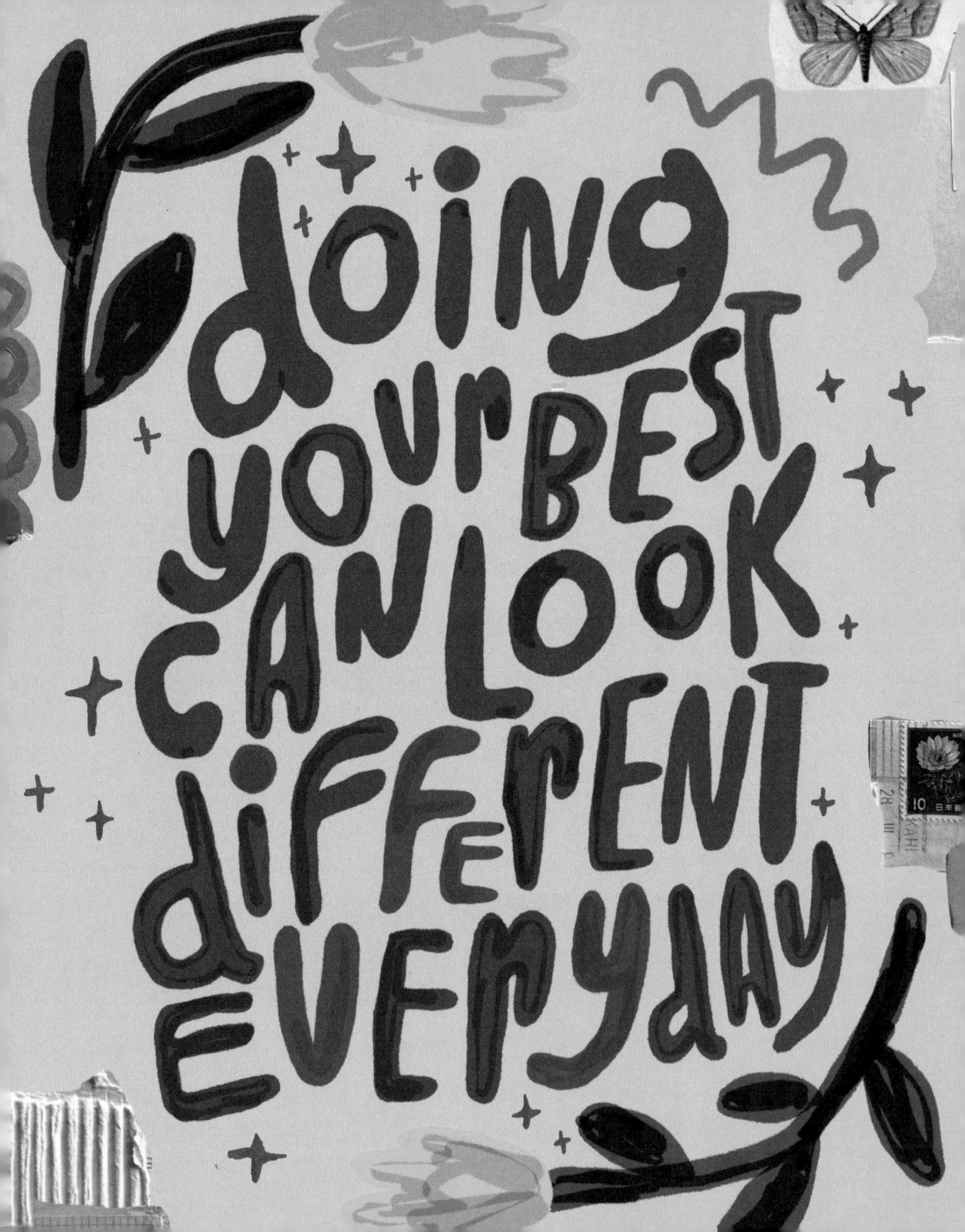
doing your best
can look
different
everyday

Doing your Best

All we can ever do is show up as we are.

I cannot change the mistakes I've made. I cannot re-create those moments and reconfigure how I handled myself. (I really wish I could sometimes.) But I can learn and I can grow. I can do better with the things I gained from those experiences. That doesn't mean the next time I'll do it perfectly; it just means I'll do it better than I did. Becoming is a process.

SELF-AWARENESS is ActuALLy tHE wOrst

So maybe you didn't need to fully explode your life like I did to come to a place of authentic living; for your sake, I hope not. But I think in any case of growing into yourself, you will have some sense of shedding and starting over, and—let's be honest—that can be *scary*.

So when you're sitting there, legs crossed, looking at all the pieces of yourself scattered on the bedroom floor like piles of discarded clothes, it can feel extremely daunting to choose where to start and what putting it back together will look like in practice. Is there a system? A rhythm to follow? And then you *know*. That's the part that makes self-awareness sort of . . . suck. It's like, once you realize all the work there is to do, you can't just *unknow* it. You must make the choice that living that way isn't working for you. You must make the conscious decision that you want to heal and then realize that, more than everything else, the healing starts with you.

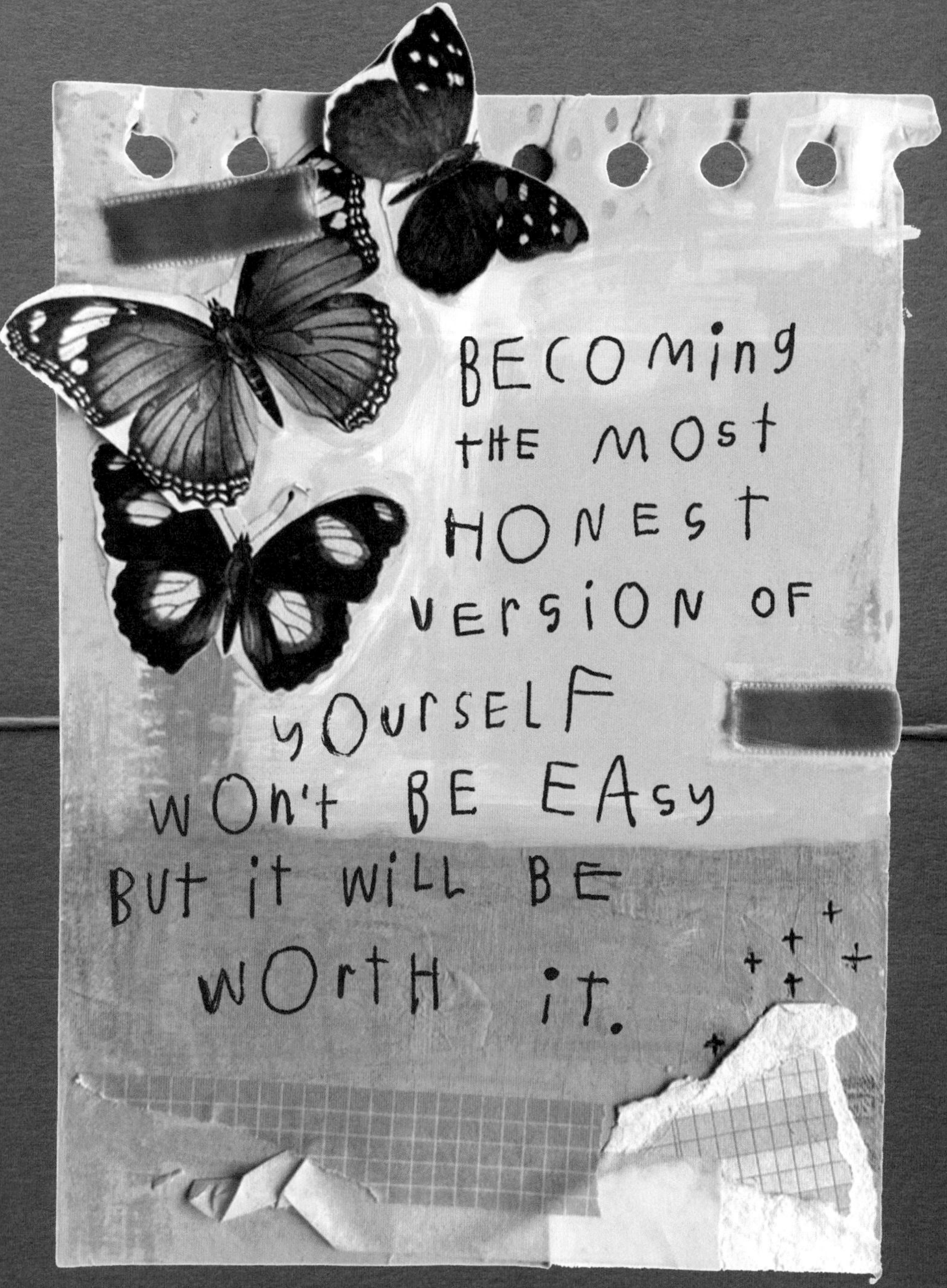
BECOMING THE MOST HONEST VERSION OF YOURSELF WON'T BE EASY BUT IT WILL BE WORTH IT.

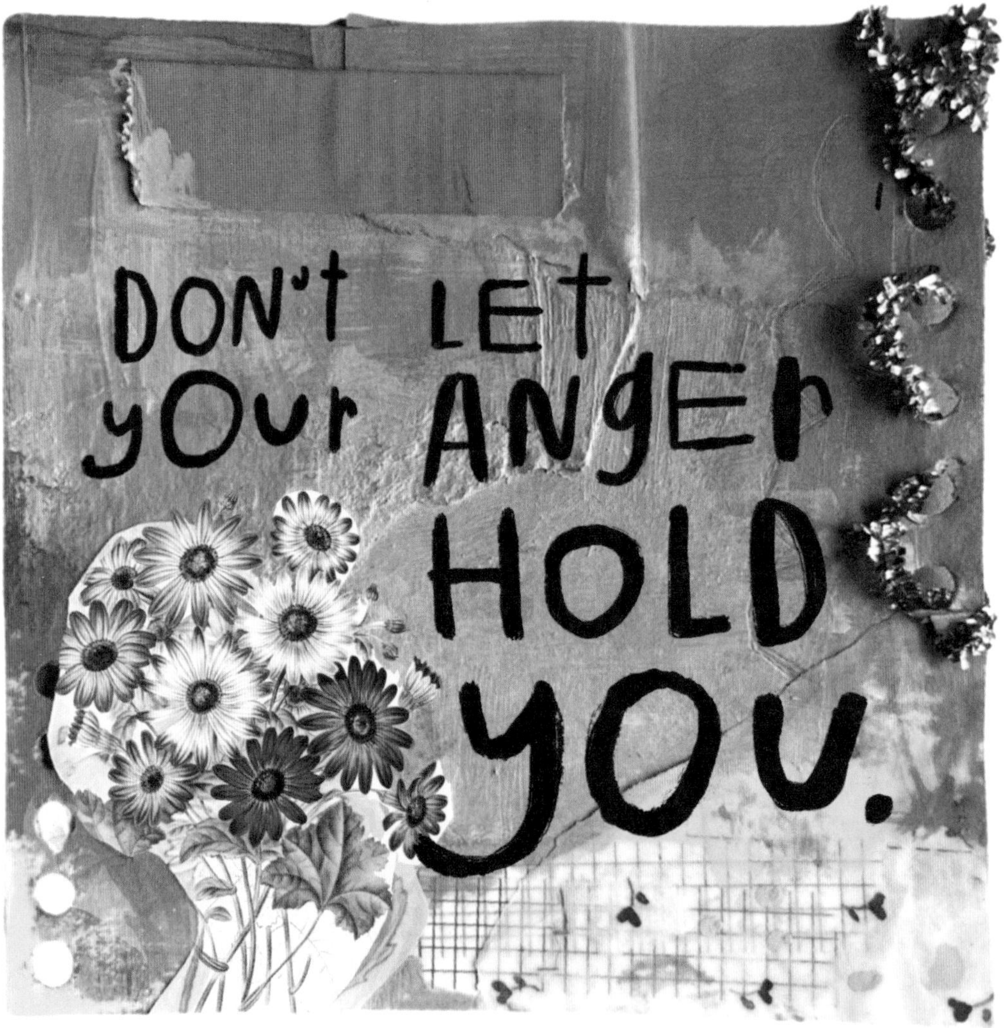
DON'T LET
YOUR ANGER
HOLD
YOU.

BiG MaD

For most of my life, anger and I have usually been strangers. Not that I didn't have situations or relationships that made me feel angry growing up; I did. But anytime I felt my body temperature rise or my fists clench, there was a fear that came on just as quickly: the fear of *Where the hell do I put this feeling?* Anger was an emotion served to me boiling hot in every form: yelling, hitting, screaming, chasing, punching. It's like some parents tell you to be cautious of the stove and then throw the pot at you, ya know? There was no way to know what could set the timer off; it could be tattling on my brother or something as simple as asking my teacher to sign a permission slip. I learned quickly that there was no space for my own anger simply because it wasn't safe. I couldn't outrun or hide from the anger I felt coming toward me, so I would learn to control the anger within me by doing what I knew how to do best: I stuffed it down. I would feel the discomfort rise in my body, and instead of letting it out, I would dig a little hole inside myself and bury it. What I couldn't see obviously couldn't hurt me, right? I became so good at masking this emotion even from myself that I started to believe it was just not part of my emotional profile anymore. My dissociation from my anger, I thought, was a masterful assertion of will and self-control, but instead it was most likely a cause of my digestive issues and blocked chakras. But beyond physically and spiritually clogging my systems, it became painfully evident to me that I couldn't hide from my anger. That shit had taken root, and roots are not easy to pull up. My anger began to grow and to escape through small cavities in ways that made me confused—like, where was this coming from?

Anger is a response that usually triggers our protection system. It's often a secondary emotion that can be covering up other things we're feeling or experiencing. To understand that, I decided to illustrate some things about anger, because sometimes I retain information better when it's presented to me in a visually attractive way.

IF YOU KNEW ME, YOU DON'T KNOW ME. I'VE GROWN, CHANGED, EVOLVED. I LISTEN TO MY SPIRIT & HEART AS THEY LEAD ME. I KNOW I CANNOT FIND MYSELF IN OTHERS. I BELONG DEEPLY TO MYSELF.

TAKE time tO BE PrOUD OF HOW FAr YOU'VE COME.

FLY ON ANYWAY

The season of mass exodus came quickly after my coming out. Not only was I dealing with my identity crisis, dismantling my marriage, trying to keep it together for my kids, and losing my only stable income as a nanny; one by one I lost most of my friends. I would cringe when my phone made a noise because I knew it was likely another angry text or hard conversation awaiting me. I wanted to stand in my truth but I didn't want to fight, which mostly led to my being a punching bag or avoiding conversations altogether. I began to understand how conditional friendship and love can be. What do you do when your lifeboat of community has left you to drown? It seems there's a communally approved checklist of things most people are willing to stay and support you through. When you break out of those boxes of societally instilled norms, people start to get really distressed. Your new light shines on them

and it may expose some of the tender stuff in them that they aren't ready or willing to face. I'll tell you this: you're gonna have to choose to shine anyway.

My therapist explained it to me like this: It's like you're a bird that's always had a broken wing. People got used to you being a little broken; it made them comfortable, and they knew how you fit into their lives that way. But then you did all this work and this healing and you're like, "Hey, guys, I can fly again"—and instead of encouraging or supporting you they say, "No, no, you can't fly!" and you plead with them and say, "No, really, I can fly again! Watch!" And you try to fly, and they may even swat you out of the air, and for some reason they think they're protecting you or maybe protecting themselves. But, either way, your flying signifies something they're actually not ready to face. It may mean a change they don't feel prepared enough to confront. So you must be okay with flying on without them.

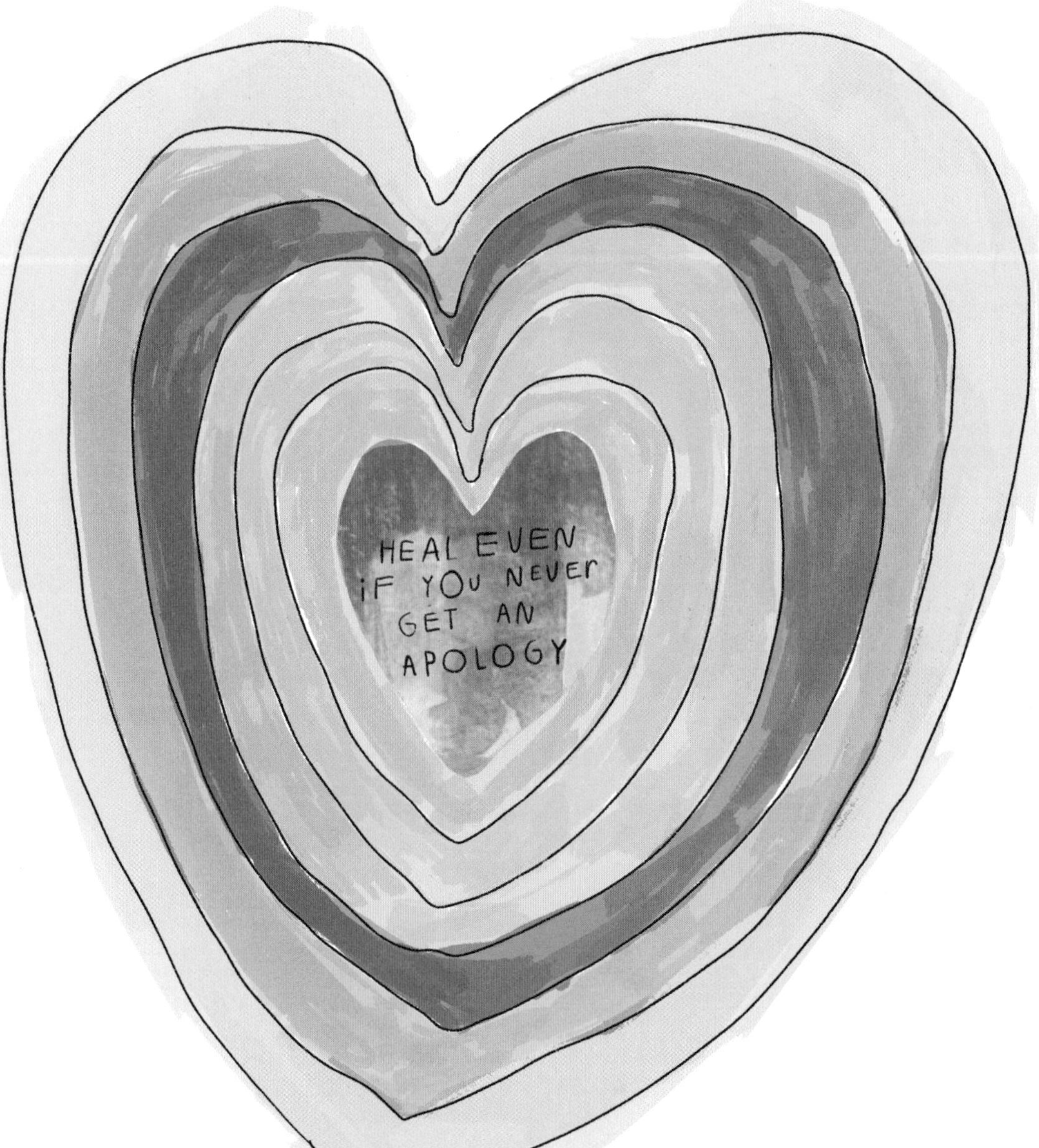
HEAL EVEN
IF YOU NEVER
GET AN
APOLOGY

taking responsibility for your own

1.5-2.0"

larva   Virginia Ctenucha

OWN

LiFE

WiLL SET YOU FREE.

Detroit MI

rADicAL rESPONSiBiLity

The morning light piercing the closed blinds casts shadows across my plants and trinkets. I try to imprint this image in my mind. I can't tell if my brain is foggy or the light is just diffused to the point where I can see dust particles floating. On days like this, I start to realize the weight of my decision to choose to show up for my life. It means I must be present in a way I don't always love to be. It means deciding I'm not only going to live but I'm also going to be responsible for myself and my life. It means my feelings and experiences are valid, but it doesn't mean they're fact. I had to choose to stop blaming and projecting those feelings and experiences on everyone else and own how I moved forward in my life.

We must be accountable to ourselves.

NOTE ON STAYING SMALL

I recently found a letter of recommendation my high school teacher wrote for me for college; we're talking an almost twenty-year-old letter. Part of me wondered how that vibrant person they wrote of became so colorless for some time in the years that followed. I kept shrinking myself down, folding myself like origami, solidifying each fold with the crease of expectation I felt I had to uphold until I was pleated into a shape that could be presented outwardly as beautiful, as art. I did this over and over until I folded a box to keep me comfortable, each side sturdy in its handcrafted security. I did well in these worlds, the ones with guidelines and instructions to keep me safe . . . or what I perceived as

DON'T RUN AWAY FROM HARD CONVERSATIONS. THEY WILL BE WAITING for YOU.

ONE OF THE HARDEST LESSONS I'VE EVER HAD TO LEARN is YOUR "STUFF" WILL FOLLOW YOU UNTIL YOU DEAL WITH IT.

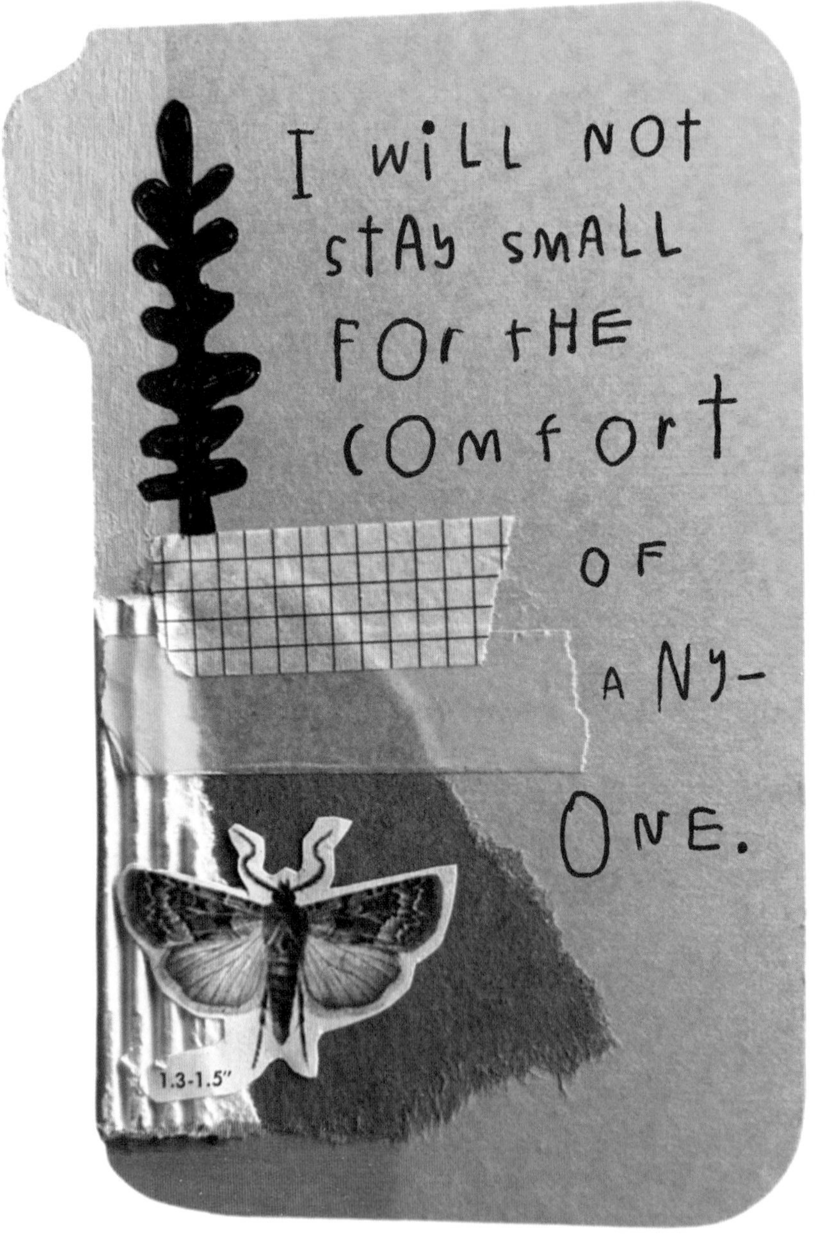
I will not
stay small
for the
comfort
of
any-
one.
1.3-1.5″

safe. I was slow to make decisions, consulting the rule books and those around me to validate that I was making the "right" decisions. I learned to doubt myself and my ability to hear and know what decisions were best for me. I couldn't act on what aligned with my soul.

Not trusting your own inner voice is a scary place to be.

I spent my entire first childbirth incessantly apologizing for being in so much pain. I thought I was being a wimp and not handling the pain as I should. I didn't have a guide to laboring properly in public, so instead of just feeling and experiencing whatever was coming, I tried to be small.

Trying to suppress the feeling that I had disappointed my midwives when I decided to get the epidural, wondering if they were mad at me or if they just thought I was a huge baby failure who couldn't handle the thing I was biologically designed to do. I cared so much; too much. I cared so much about how everyone perceived me that I didn't even know how to perceive myself.

for this next part, Let's focus on joy

So, yes, living authentically can be a messy, chaotic, roller-coaster ride of highs and lows. As can healing, finding your voice, making boundaries, and finding peace. But let's not forget about the thing that makes the wild ride worth taking: The real reason to live an honest, authentic life is to fully experience *joy*. Every evolution I've undergone in my life has enabled me to more deeply and wholly interact with and rest in my joy. My trauma and conditioning always kept me on guard, telling me not to indulge in joy too completely because joy is fleeting. Can you imagine living like that? Or, even worse, have you been living like that? I lived that way for too long, not allowing myself to be present in my joy for fear of it being ripped away from me, never savoring my moments of happiness and contentment because my anxiety was steadily whispering that they would never last. I feel sadness for the moments

I missed, when my body was physically present but my mind was checking to see if there was trouble on the horizon. The more I peel back the layers of myself and come to terms with who I am and who I want to be, the less time I spend looking over my shoulder. The more stable I feel in myself, the more I recognize and understand that my joy can never be taken. I may not always be conscious of it—sometimes other emotions have to take center stage—but my joy is my resistance. It's why I will overcome again and again and again. The more I let myself feel it, the more resilience I have for another trying season. So now I savor my joy. I let the flavor flood my mouth and take my time consuming it. I sink into it like a soothing bath of salts and oils. I let it replenish me. I hold it loosely because I do not fear its disappearance. Your joy can always be found. It's in the first sips of morning coffee and the hugs from your kids after school; it's in the belly laughs alongside friends who see you; it's in the crisp air before winter and the rays of the sun at the first spring thaw; it's the song that you've listened to thirty times on repeat and a text from the one who fills your stomach with butterflies. I hope you look for it, I hope you seize it, I hope you breathe it in.

EVER FORWARD

So the general burning question is: Do I still believe in God? If you're asking if I believe in a God that was created and rewritten by white men to shame, control, and oppress, then no. No, I do not. I have crystals on every ledge and bookshelf in my home. I always notice when the clock says 4:44, and I do very much care what your astrological sign is. (Let's be real: if you have your whole chart handy, I want to see it, and also I love you.) I have multiple tarot decks and mind the moon cycles. Call me woo-woo, call me a witch, whatever it all is that helps keep me grounded and self-reflective. But if you're asking if I believe there is something bigger than us—call it God, the universe, Mother Earth, the divine, whatever it may be—then yes. I think at the end of the day what I really believe in is hope.

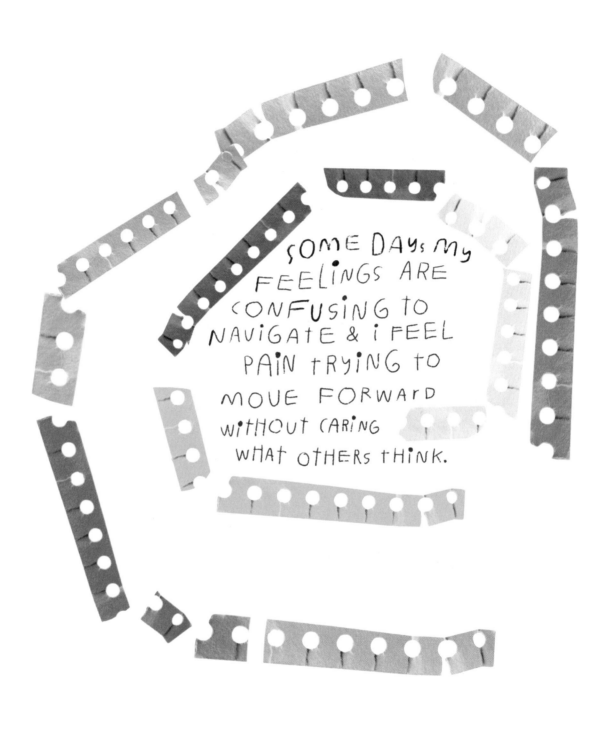

SOME DAYs my
FEELINGS ARE
CONFUSING to
NAVIGATE & i FEEL
PAIN tRYING to
MOVE FORWARD
WithOUT CARING
WHAt OtHERs tHiNK.

tiny rituals
FOR HOPE

LIGHT A CANDLE

PLANT SOMETHING &
WATCH IT grow

WRITE DOWN FUTURE
HOPES & DREAMS

THE STORIES WE KNOW

LEAVING BEHIND THE STORIES WE ~~HOLD~~ HOLD ABOUT OURSELVES & OUR LIVES WILL ALLOW US TO STEP INTO LIVING OUR TRUTH. ♡

THE StORiES WE KNOW

When we go through things, our stories are etched in our mind and replayed to us throughout our lives when situations that trigger those narratives come up. Being able to leave behind certain parts of those stories will bring us freedom. I'm not saying to forget things that happened to you, but, for example, if your parents weren't around or even just emotionally unavailable, you might have told yourself that you were unlovable. Now, as a grown adult human person, when someone doesn't answer your call or is working late and can't hang out, that idea might come to mind again and start to make you feel dejected when, in reality, your friend might just be busy, and it has nothing to do with your ability to be loved. It's important to understand that some of these notions may have even kept us safe in our childhoods, but now they hold us back from true connection and healing.

Your story isn't over.

Maybe we are the sum of our experiences, but we are not defined by them. Our past doesn't have to dictate where we go in the future; it's just a map of where we've come from. Rewrite, edit, and keep going: your story is a work of art in process.

chicken therapy

A few years ago I started raising chickens. That's right: little feathered descendants of dinosaurs on our small city plot. I had a lot of fancy dreams about farms when I was growing up. I would read blogs and see women in long, flowing dresses tending gardens and picking vegetables they'd grown from seeds before the spring truly broke. Windswept hair that looked like they just got a blowout from an overpriced salon and name-brand clogs that cost as much as my grocery bill. They made pie crust from scratch and filled it with blackberries they picked on their morning meditation walk. Their houses were painted all white and filled with woven baskets, wood grain, and eucalyptus. I so deeply wanted to be these women. They seemed like they lived a life of ease. They always seemed to convey a level of contentment that I desperately longed for but could never attain. There were many reasons why this wasn't the life I ended up living. One, I'm a city person forever. I find comfort in the noise and chaos and the sirens going off in the distance. I like knowing that if I screamed, someone would probably hear me and couldn't just throw my body in a cornfield (dark, I know), and the idea of having no streetlights or neighbors nearby is actually terrifying to me. Two, I'm bad at gardening and cooking and baking. Okay, I'm not *bad* at any of those things, but because of my ADHD I'm very forgetful and get bored really easily. I'm great at planting things and terrible at remembering to water them. I'm great at cooking, but if the recipe says anything about taking more than forty-five minutes to prepare, I would rather eat cereal. Three, I aesthetically love the idea of a minimalist, airy, bright, clean home, but I'm a person who paints the mantel neon pink while their partner and kids are asleep, so that went out the window, too. But chickens—they never left my mind. I used to spend a lot of time traveling to visit friends in Portland, Oregon. I would walk around and see bite-size mini farms on a busy city street. It felt like maybe pieces of my dream could be reimagined. When I bought my house, I hadn't even closed before a friend of mine asked if I wanted to adopt three of her hens. I had absolutely no idea what I was doing but excitedly agreed, purchased a coop-in-a-box, and instantly became a first-time homeowner and a chicken mom in one fell swoop. An irrational thing for an autistic/ADHD human with commitment issues

to do: getting a living creature to care for that requires you to go *outside* and do monotonous tasks. I was absolutely intimidated by the idea that I might completely fail or, even worse, just end up hating this last little piece of my dream of a rural life. Slowly the days turned to weeks and the weeks to months. I found myself creating new rituals that revolved around tending to my "girls." I spent time shoveling space for them to walk in the snow and noticed myself grabbing extra cartons of blueberries and bags of kale on trips to the grocery store. They would sit on my lap when I sat outside with my morning coffee and follow me to the back screen door, waiting for me to throw the vegetable scraps onto the deck. They reminded me to slow down. To listen to the melodic crunch of the leaves under us as we all walked through the yard. To breathe in the fresh air and get myself out of my head and into my body. They showed me companionship that wasn't based on anything other than mutual care. I tended to them, and they provided for us. It was so simple yet so symbiotic. Every day I would thank them for their eggs as I pulled them out of the snow-warped nesting box in the cheap coop I had assembled, which now was slightly askew. The girls didn't require much: just showing up. I didn't have to do anything elaborate to earn or keep our cooperative union intact. It reminded me of how simple and innate it can be to take care of each other—how broken pieces can become new dreams, and it's those mosaics we will use to line the path forward.

WE TAKE CARE OF EACH OTHER.

. CONCLUSION .

So there it is: an untidy, unconventional account of my experiences, stories, and big feels. Do I feel a little exposed? Yes. Was it worth it? I really think so. Because I hope maybe you can see yourself here. I hope maybe you felt a little more seen and a little less alone in this whole being-a-person thing we're all navigating. I hope maybe you can offer yourself more gentleness as you move through your own becoming. I want us all to be the most authentic, healed versions of ourselves. I want us all to know we're living our lives as fully and freely as we could ever imagine. I want us all to win. xo

...... ACKNOWLEDGMENTS.

I acknowledge that by the time you're reading this, I will have already learned and expanded past the person I was on these pages. That even though this is a tangible immortalization of my thoughts and experiences, I accept that, like me, life is fluid and ever changing. I understand that this is my story from my perspective and experience, and it may differ from how other s saw and felt and experienced things. I hold space for it all.

I acknowledge all the painful, messy parts of my story and take responsibility for the ways I, too, have fucked up.

I want to acknowledge you, the reader, follower, human, for being in spaces with me as I grew up and grew into myself over the last ten years online. This book is so much for you and your own becoming, too.

Kate and Ronnie, thank you for seeing a book in me before I ever could. Thanks for pushing me to places and teaching me things during the process. Thank you for making space for life and aching and charting a new course when needed. Thanks for always putting Jess the person before Jess the author. Your tenderness has made this magical. I'll never be able to fully express what it feels like to have people you trust in your corner while working on a project like this.

I acknowledge that I wouldn't be here or have written this book without Joanne, my therapist of six years, who helped me through my childhood trauma, coming out, two divorces, my ADHD diagnosis, a suicide attempt, friendship pains, autism testing, and learning to love and forgive myself. It feels just right that your retiring comes with the finishing of this book. Your blue couch was my safe place. I hope to see you on the other side, in the world as regular people someday.

To my friends who have stood alongside me, held me, watched my kids, brought me coffee, made sure I ate, and celebrated every tiny step of this process: you are my family, my community, my home. Khaleef, Sarah, Champagne, Danny, Sofia, Jenna, Nae Nae, and Kenny. And all the joy brought by my auntie and those with extended auntie privileges Eli, Zeke, Haper Kate, Mabel, Maslo, Niamh, Mae, Zoë, and Margaux.

Rachel, thank you for your friendship in every evolution. You are such a precious soul. Thank you for allowing me to share your photography in this book and on the cover. I will always love collaborating on life with you.

Bex, your family and your friendship saved my life. I love you.

Em, since fifth grade, thanks for knowing me deeply, calling me out, and loving me hard.

To my sister, Pook: you are my best friend. The dream was to survive. Now, I get to pull up next to you at the pick-up loop as we pick our babies up from school. It's everything. You were with me when this book was a glimmer, an email of interest we read in the community space we built, wondering if this was real life. It will always be us against everything. Thank you for always having my back. I love you forever.

Miles and Sawyer, you will never understand how grateful I am that the universe trusted me to be your mom. You are the light in every darkness. I know someday you will read and understand so much of our family's story that maybe I wasn't ready to tell you fully, but I want you to know that you were always loved, kept safe, and cherished. You were always my reason to keep going.

Nan, a therapist once told me that you can go through all sorts of hardships, but if you have even one person whom you know is *for* you, you can overcome almost anything. I have always known that person was you. Your endless capacity to give to our entire family over a lifetime is honestly borderline insane, and yet I'm so grateful. Thanks for fostering my creativity, giving me a home, and having my back on every crazy project I kept you up late at the kitchen table to help me with. I love you (and Papa!) with everything I am.

Sarina, your love championed this book. Thank you for helping me use my voice. Thanks for wanting a wild, unconventional life with me and making it happen every day. Someday, we'll create a new word for love. There's no one else I would tolerate farting on me when I spoon them. I love you.